AFRICA

NATURAL SPIRIT OF THE AFRICAN CONTINENT

AFRICA

NATURAL SPIRIT OF THE AFRICAN CONTINENT

Gill Davies

PaRragon

Bath · New York · Singapore · Hong Kong · Cologne · Delhi · Melbourne

First published by Parragon in 2007

Parragon Publishing

Queen Street House

4 Queen Street

Bath BA1 1HE, UK

Copyright © Parragon Books Ltd 2007

Designed, produced, and packaged by Stonecastle Graphics Limited

Text by Gill Davies

Designed by Paul Turner and Sue Pressley

Edited by Philip de Ste. Croix

ISBN 978-1-4054-8672-9

Printed in China

Page 1: *Samburu girl, near Samburu National Reserve, Kenya.*

Pages 2-3: *The largest mammal migration in the world is that of the Serengeti wildebeest. Huge herds of these antelopes congregate on the East African savannahs, grazing the seasonal grasses until drought and depletion force them to move from the plains to open woodland in search of food.*

Pages 4-5: *A female white rhino and her young calf grazing in a game reserve in KwaZulu-Natal province, South Africa.*

CONTENTS

INTRODUCTION

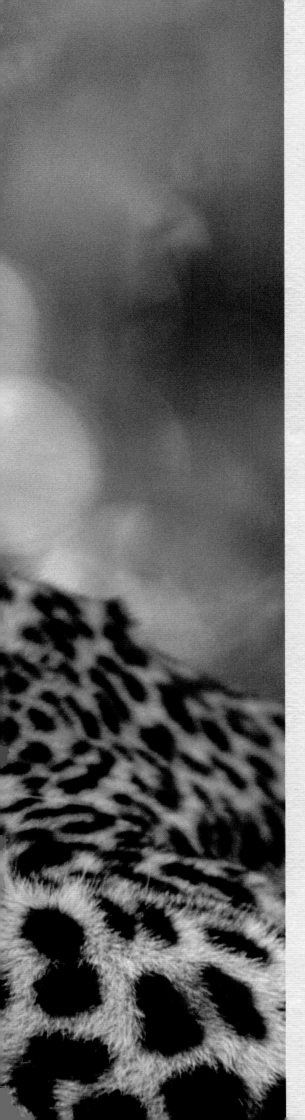

Africa … the very name sets the imagination on fire. Many vivid images compete to take precedence – the savannah baking under deep blue skies where lions doze in the purple shadows of tree and scrub; herds of wildebeest massing on the plains, their strange musical lowing rippling across the still air; monkeys swinging through an emerald jungle canopy; crocodile snouts – a dimpled threat in pools where huge hippo glisten, wallow, and bake. An outline of camels carves a sharp edge against the desert horizon; the River Nile glides majestically past ancient temples and pyramids; the tumultuous crash of the Victoria Falls, dizzy with rainbows. A proud Zulu warrior stands tall, bare feet planted firmly on African soil and history. The robes of a Maasai herdsman make a distant scarlet flash on a dusty road. Somewhere, along a red-baked track, comes a scamper of warthogs – shiny, plump backsides soon scurrying for cover. Later, as the hot day dips toward dark, a thorn tree etches its contorted silhouette against a crimson sunset. Soon the trill of cicadas charges the sudden swift dusk and then, as the velvet dark sweeps down, glittering hyena eyes ring a night camp. All this is Africa. All this, and so much more…

This book explores the multiple layers of the many nations, the tribes, and history of Africa. The story of humankind can be traced back to Olduvai Gorge in Tanzania, often called the 'Cradle of Mankind' – since this steep-sided ravine in the Great Rift Valley is where some of the oldest ever human remains and tools have been found, dating back to about 2.6 million years ago.

Africa is a vast continent, an almost triangular landmass with islands scattered about its crinkled edges. This grand tour sweeps first across the North – from the Mediterranean fringe across the Atlas Mountains and the Sahara Desert to Egypt and the Red Sea, Niger, and Mali. Thence our exploration gradually

meanders south, through many nations and habitats, to the countries of Nigeria, Zambia, Kenya, and Madagascar, until it reaches South Africa and the Cape of Good Hope.

During this journey from north to south, in each of the five sections the focus homes in ever closer – from nation and people to landscape and terrain – to explore mountain, sea, lake, savannah, forest, and river; and then to take an even closer look into the trees and bush, shifting sands, leaves, grasses, and gleaming waters. Gradually the life of Africa is revealed in all its diversity and glory. While no single volume of this scale can encompass each and every creature that runs and hops, slithers and flies, and marches through Africa, or swims around its coast, a good many are revealed here – from the smallest frog and termite to the great elephant and blue whale, from soaring eagles high in the sky to manta rays rippling through deep seas.

This little 'drop in the ocean' can never do justice to the great continent that is Africa. This is an immense place with countless threads interwoven into its tapestry. I do hope, however, that this book conveys the magic, encapsulates some of the atmosphere, and brings a few of the continent's beautiful and amazing creatures into sharper focus, and that the very special Spirit of Africa is conjured from the continent to breathe life into these pages too.

Page 6: A leopard in Mala Mala game reserve, South Africa. The sleek coat of each leopard bears a unique pattern of dark spots and 'rosettes' that help its camouflage.
Page 7: Sunset and silhouette – gemsbok in the Kalahari Gemsbok National Park, South Africa.

Above: As the moon rises in Botswana, it highlights the contorted shape of an ancient baobab tree.
Right: African elephants live in a complex matriarchal society normally composed of some eight to 15 related members and led by a dominant cow.

NORTH AFRICA

This area of enormous contrasts lies close to latitudes where the Tropic of Cancer extends in a dotted line across the map. It encompasses the Mediterranean fringe, including Tunisia and Algeria, the high peaks and fertile valleys of the Atlas Mountains, the vast sweep of the Sahara, the banks of the Nile, and the Red Sea coast.

The Mediterranean edge

North Africa is edged by the glittering Mediterranean Sea where dry, hot summers and relatively warm winters have long made parts of Morocco and Tunisia popular tourist destinations. The coastal plains provide arable land fed by water from inland mountain streams where local people raise crops. Inland are fertile valleys where citrus fruit and olives flourish. The high sharp peaks of the Atlas Mountains trap the moist air that soars up from the Atlantic and Mediterranean – and when the clouds meet the high peaks the ensuing rainfall pelts down to fill streams and rivers in the mountains. Because all this moisture usually pours out of the clouds on the coastal side of the Atlas Mountains, the Sahara Desert that lies on the other side of the peaks remains dry and inhospitable.

The Atlas Mountains

The upward thrust of the Atlas Mountains separates the Mediterranean and Atlantic coastlines from the Sahara Desert. On the map, their skeletal ridge traces a line beside the desert sand, snaking along for 1500 miles (2400km) with its final miniature flourish being the sharp outcrop of the Rock of Gibraltar, famous for the 300 or so tailless Barbary macaques *(Macaca sylvanus)* that live there and which make the odd trip into town for a change of scenery. The Atlas system consists of the Middle Atlas, Anti-Atlas, and High Atlas ranges – where Toubkal Mountain in Morocco rises to 13,671ft (4167m). In geological terms, these are quite new peaks, created when the African and American continental plates collided about 300 million years ago – and they were once far higher than the Himalayas. The indigenous populations include Berbers in Morocco and Arabs in Algeria. Anti-Atlas has both rugged landscape and fertile valleys. Once there were forests and beautiful cedar trees but these have long been depleted.

Page 10: The Tuareg people of the Sahara Desert in Mali wear blue robes and indigo turbans. They even stain their skin blue.
Page 11: A Tunisian straw hut with its door painted the traditional blue color.

Above: Barbary macaques live in troops (usually comprising about 24 individuals) and are social animals that spend some 20 percent of the day grooming one another.
Right: The Berber village of Ait Toukshine in Morocco. The Atlas mountain range separates the Mediterranean and Atlantic coastlines from the Sahara Desert.

Top: A gnarled old olive tree. Tunisians once exchanged their jewels and dowries for these precious trees that provided 'the black pearls.'
Above: A strange landscape of palm trees and petrified sand dunes in Tunisia.

North Africa's sub-regions comprise the Maghrib – Arabic for 'where the Sun sets,' including western areas such as Morocco, Algeria, and Tunisia – and the Mashriq, 'where the Sun rises,' denoting lands farther east, such as Libya and Egypt. However, the terms seem to be interpreted differently depending on where you are at sunrise and sunset!

People and farming

Many millions of people live here, including Berbers and Arabs – in what might seem a harsh environment but which in fact offers some surprising riches. Farmers herd cattle and many keep sheep, camels, and goats – as do nomads. Herds are moved from one pasture area to another; the locals take advantage of different growing seasons by driving their livestock up and down the mountains to make the most of summer grasses and winter pastures. Farmers grow olives, dates, figs, and – in areas where there are steep mountain slopes – plants may be grown in rock terraces that retain a little soil and rainwater. North African crops include wheat, barley, grapes, and olives. Along the fertile banks of the river Nile many citrus fruits, dates, and vegetables are grown. Egypt (where the livestock includes water buffalo) is renowned for its cotton. Other crops include peanuts in Libya, vines in Morocco, and oats in Algeria, while Tunisia produces tomatoes, sugar beets, and almonds. In the Western Sahara, lush fruits and vegetables thrive in the rare oases.

Vanishing ways of life and wildlife

Nomads travel great distances, often following animal migration routes in search of food and water, or they may be traders transporting products from one area to another. This is a fast vanishing way of life, as in recent years most of the nomads have relinquished their wandering status in favor of a more permanent agricultural or herding lifestyle.

North Africa supports a variety of wildlife species that flourish in this very varied range of habitats. However, many species are endangered, such as the monk seal *(Monachus monachus)* – sadly far fewer now cavort in the Mediterranean along Algeria's coastline. Barbary deer *(Cervus elaphus barbarus)* in Morocco, Algeria, and Tunisia, and the Nile crocodile *(Crocodylus niloticus)* in Egypt are also now rare, while the brown Atlas bear *(Ursus crowtheri)* disappeared due to habitat destruction in the Moroccan mountains in the 1870s. Hartebeest *(Alcelaphus buselaphus)* have been hunted to extinction. The Barbary (or Atlas) lion *(Panthera leo leo)* was a fierce, beautiful beast, much valued by the Ancient Romans, but intense hunting and habitat loss finally eradicated this creature by 1922.

The Sahara Desert

The dominant feature of North Africa is the Sahara Desert covering an area of some 3.3 million square miles (8.6 million km²) from its western Atlantic edge to the Nile delta and the Red Sea. Temperatures can soar to 130°F (54°C) during the day and then may plummet down to below freezing at night. Rainfall is rare and comes in sudden bursts that can cause flash floods. Sand storms sometimes whip

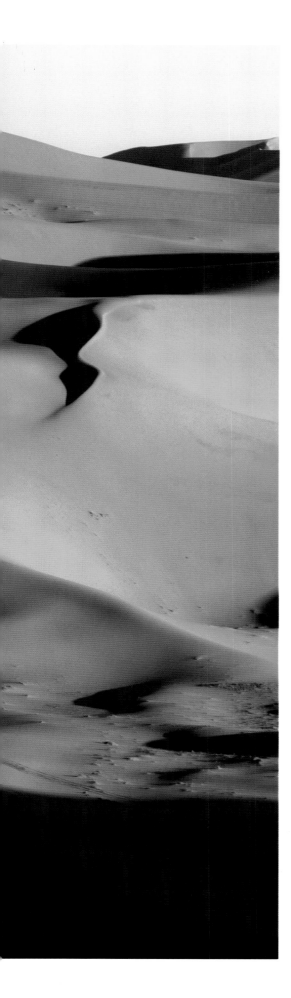

across the land, carrying huge quantities of sand far across the continent and sometimes even into Europe.

There are spectacular high sand dunes. The world's highest dunes are in the Algerian part of the Sahara; at 1525ft (465m) they are taller than New York's Empire State Building. Here too are massive 'sand seas,' hard rock clay steppes, gravel beds, and dry mountains. The Sahara is also dotted with oases, where small fertile pockets thrive on the water drawn from underground mountain springs and streams. Crops such as dates and figs grow around oases and desert travelers and herders can find a precious brief respite from the hostile environment. Desert foxes are found in the Sahara along with hares, gazelles, and the jerboa, a small leaping rodent about 2-6in (5-15cm) long with a 3-10in (8-25cm) long tail. It looks rather like a mouse but one with a long tufted tail and extremely long, thin hind legs that enable this tiny creature to leap high to escape from predators. The lesser Egyptian jerboa *(Jaculus jaculus)* survives the arid desert climate by not needing to drink at all; instead this nocturnal creature relies on its food to provide enough moisture for survival and goes into a state of semi-hibernation during the hottest summer months.

Left: *Orange sand dunes scoured by wind and bathed in deep shadows in the Sahara Desert, Morocco.*

Above: *Date palm trees ring a desert oasis in South Tunisia.*

Egypt and the Nile

Egypt is a land of contrasts, with its fertile strip looking like an emerald border to the ribbon of the Nile. For centuries the river has flooded every year, bringing fertile soils washed all the way down from Ethiopia and Sudan to be deposited across the Egyptian flood plain. In 1902 the first Aswan Dam was completed, followed in 1970 by the new High Dam that now controls the flow of water to irrigate farms all along the Nile plain, a green strip of fertility in an otherwise barren terrain. In its northern delta the Nile spreads its fluid fingers in tendrils that look, on the map, like the head of a lotus flower. Here farmers grow corn, rice, and wheat.

The Nile slides through a varied landscape, through the orange sandstone hills of Nubia, past villages, palms, and tamarisk trees. Its edges are lined with low flat buildings, beaches where women wash clothes, dogs bark, and children play, dirt roads and fields where donkeys plod along laden with heavy burdens. There are fertile open plains, sandstone hills that sometimes close into gorges, and limestone cliffs. Throughout Upper and Middle Egypt the flood plain is broad, and the lush cultivation includes wheat, sugar cane, mango, and banana trees, orange and lemon groves, palm trees – and everywhere the foliage is busy with birds – turtle doves, pigeons, bee-eaters, and hoopoes.

The sacred ibis *(Threskiornis aethiopicus)* was once a common wading bird in the Nile region. An Ancient Egyptian favorite, believed to ward off serpents, it was depicted in many murals and sculptures as Thoth, the ibis-headed god of wisdom, and it also appeared as a hieroglyphic symbol. This bird was venerated and veritable 'cemeteries' of ibis mummies have been found at Sakkara near Cairo and at Hermopolis in middle Egypt. Now only an occasional visitor to North

Above: *A sacred ibis. The ancient Egyptians believed that Thoth (the gods' scribe) came to Earth in the form of this attractive bird.*

Right: *Stout colonnades in Luxor. Ancient Egyptian decoration included such creatures as birds, crocodiles, and scarab beetles.*

Africa, it has not bred in Egypt since the 1800s but still lives in sub-Saharan Africa in coastal lagoons, marshes, mudflats, damp lowlands, and flooded areas where it eats fish, frogs, and insects. It will also scavenge about in garbage tips whenever possible! The sacred ibis has white plumage with dark feathers on the rump and black legs, head, neck, and bill.

Sacred creatures

The ancestors of crocodiles appeared on Earth some 230 million years ago – since when these fierce reptiles have changed very little. The Nile crocodile *(Crocodylus niloticus)* lives in many parts of Africa as well as in the southern reaches of the river after which it is named. It inhabits larger rivers, estuaries, lakes, and swamps, where, depending upon its location, it enjoys a diet of fish, antelope, zebras, buffaloes, and nesting birds. This is another creature that was worshipped by the Ancient Egyptians who even raised temples to honor the crocodile god, Sobek. Since the Nile was then full of these ferocious reptiles, it would have made sense to try and appease them through worship. Even today Nile crocodiles are thought to kill as many as a thousand people every year. The mother crocodile, however, shows a more tender aspect. She carefully covers her clutches of eggs with vegetation that generates heat as it rots so keeping the nest temperature just right. Meanwhile she stays on guard and then, alerted by their chirruping, helps her babies to hatch. Finally, she collects the squirming, snapping youngsters in her great toothy jaws and carries them to the safety of the water where she continues to keep an eye on them for some two months or more.

The scarab or dung beetle *(Scarabaeus sacer)* spends a good part of its busy life finding dung pats left in the wake of grazing herds of livestock, and rolling bits of them away. The beetles stand on their front feet and push the ball (which can be considerably bigger than they are) with their back feet. Then they dig a hole and bury the ball of dung inside it. It will serve as food and, in the breeding season, the female lays an egg on top of the ball. When the egg hatches, the larva grows inside the dung ball, munching away until it pupates and hatches as a new, hungry adult. By breaking up the dung and burying it, scarab beetles also help to fertilize the land.

The Ancient Egyptians believed scarab beetles to be sacred, their golden round shape a symbol of immortality and the Sun god. The rolling of the dung ball was taken as a representation of how the Sun appeared to cross above the Earth each day to be reborn at dawn. The scarab was often carved on precious monuments and in ornate stones to be worn as official seals or jewelry, or kept as lucky charms to ward off evil.

Left: Feluccas on the Nile at Aswan, Egypt, below the mausoleum enshrining the white marble tomb of the Aga Khan. On his birthday in 1945, he was weighed in diamonds – a treasure which he then shared among his followers.

Opposite: A limestone relief of Tuthmosis III in Luxor Museum. Called the 'Napoleon of Ancient Egypt,' this fine military campaigner became pharaoh in around 1504BC.

Above: A camel at Giza. The Great Pyramid of Khufu (or Cheops) near Cairo is the oldest (and only surviving) structure named as one of the Seven Wonders of the Ancient World.

Left: An Egyptian smokes a sheesha (hookah or water pipe) in Luxor market. Sometimes three or four hoses are attached to a single pipe to allow for communal smoking.

Top and above: A dung or scarab beetle straddles a substantial ball of dung in the course of rolling it farther along the ground before burying it. Ancient Egyptians thought this activity was like the Sun being rolled across the sky each day from dawn to dusk and regarded the scarab as sacred as a consequence. It is a symbol depicted on many of their monuments.

The Red Sea

The easternmost extremity of northern Africa is lapped by the waters of the Red Sea, an inlet of the Indian Ocean between Africa and Asia, and part of the Great Rift Valley. This is a 1200 mile (1900km) long narrow strip of marine waters with extensive shallow shelves that burgeon with corals and vivid marine life including over 1000 invertebrate species and 200 soft and hard corals. This is the world's most northerly tropical sea. The Bible tells how Moses led the Israelites across the Red Sea to freedom, helped by God's parting of the waters. Today the waters welcome scuba divers instead. Temperatures remain at 70-77°F (21-25°C) year-round and there is good visibility even at 650ft (200m) depth, which makes it all the easier to see the many superbly colored fish that inhabit these waters. Even a paddle in the shallows in the right spot can be as good as a visit to an aquarium.

Life on the coral reef

Many beautiful fish are found in the Red Sea, some of them with powerful jaws that scrape away at the algae on rocks and corals. These include the stunningly vivid angelfish that appears in many startlingly rich color combinations. The Emperor angelfish (*Pomacanthus imperator*) is especially beautiful, its fluorescent blue and emerald color finely striped with yellow.

   Parrotfish (*Sparisoma cretense*) drift along the ridges of the coral reef, riding with the tidal ebb and flow. Their front teeth have fused to form a parrot-like

Above: The Red Sea, where the North African desert meets the ocean, is truly one of the planet's most exotic and fascinating natural seascape environments. The Red Sea contains beneath its crystal blue surface an oasis of living creatures, reefs, and coral formation and its use as a highway between East and West has attracted man since the beginning of time.

Opposite: The warm waters of a Red Sea coral reef are home to numerous sea creatures. It is estimated that over 1000 invertebrate species and 200 soft and hard corals live there, and it is the world's most northerly tropical sea.

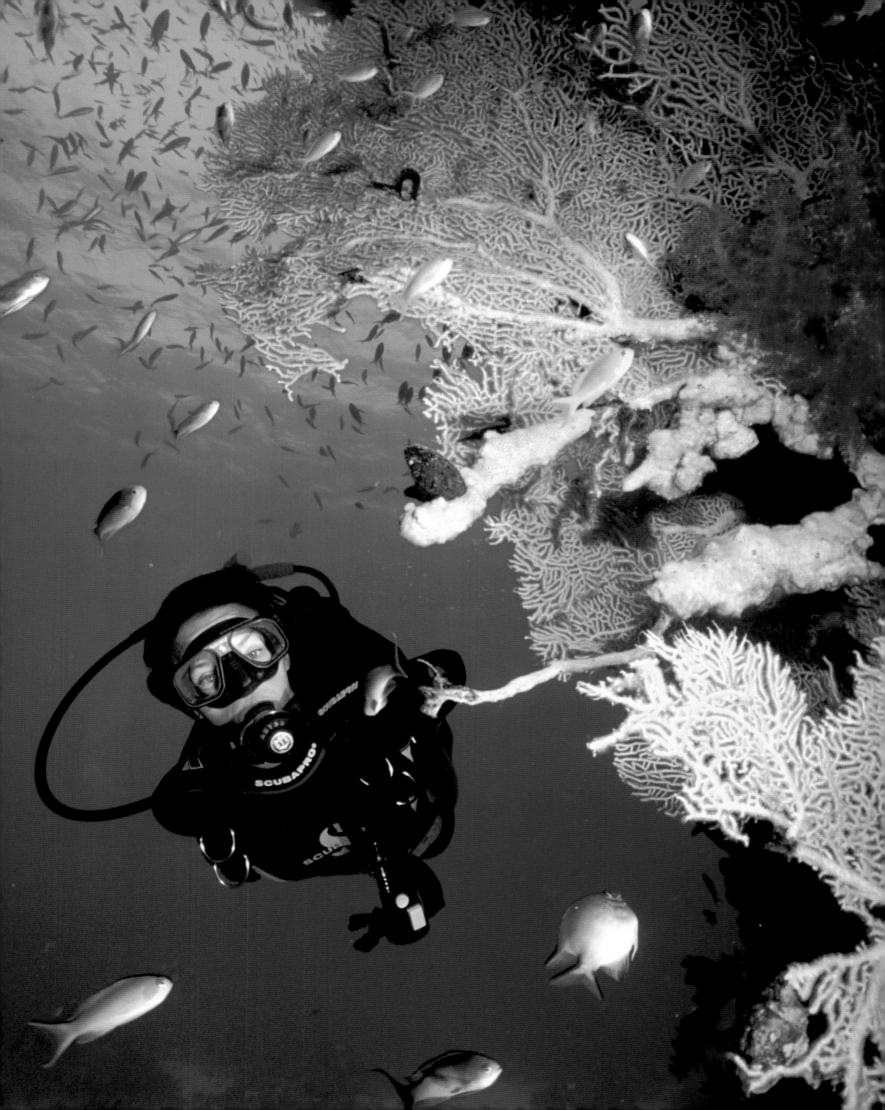

Top: *A symphony in yellow — butterfly fish, banner fish, and sweetlips are just a few of the brilliantly colored species of fish that live in the Red Sea.*

Above: *The whale shark is the largest shark (and hence the largest fish) in the world's oceans, growing up to 60ft (18m) long and weighing up to 15 tons.*

Right: *A scarlet shoal of fish below the dark shape of a manta ray, a graceful giant that can measure over 29.5ft (9m) in width.*

beak which gives rise to their name. While many are only about 18in (46cm) long, some variations on the theme can grow to up to 4ft (1.2m) in length. These fish also scrape away at the coral, loudly enough to be heard by divers. Abundant in the shallow reefs, these rich blue, green, red, and yellow fish sleep at night under ledges or in small crevices, safe inside a transparent mucous bubble that they secrete all around their rather endearing bodies to protect them from predators.

Pufferfish *(Pleuranacanthus sceleratus)* can inflate their bodies by swallowing water or air. They are also called blowfish, swellfish, globefish, or balloonfish. They swell to several times their normal size if threatened until they look like balloons with staring eyes. Their relative, the porcupine fish, uses the same trick, but with the addition of sharp spines that stick out when it inflates to strengthen its defenses. Many parts of the puffer or blowfish (liver, muscles, skin, and ovaries) contain a fierce, paralysing poison that is a thousand times deadlier than cyanide. Some species of the fish are cooked by specially-trained chefs in Japan but a few unfortunate diners have not lived to tell the fishy tale.

A fierce predator in these waters is the red lionfish *(Pterois volitans)*, also sometimes called the dragon fish or scorpion fish. They have red, brown, or black and white stripes and can change their colors and shapes. They are covered in very long spines; divers are warned to treat them with caution as they are highly venomous and can inflict excruciatingly painful – sometimes life-threatening –

wounds. The poison is for self-defense. For hunting, they rely on stealth, waiting quietly until smaller creatures approach unaware of danger; then they corner their prey with their large fins and swallow supper whole. Their mouths open wide to engulf most of the victim in one gulp. The odd tail end might still protrude for a moment or two.

Meanwhile, armed with a tiny blade or sharp plate on each side, just in front of its tail, a surgeonfish can use this weapon to defend territory. Some change color to indicate what sort of mood they are in… if provoked they will slash at other fish aggressively with their sharp, scalpel-like spines, also making side-swipes with their tails.

There are many kinds of grouper in the Red Sea, including blacktip groupers *(Epinephelus fasciatus)* that have stout bodies up to 16in (40cm) long and large mouths. Groupers lie in wait for fish, octopus, crab, or lobster and then 'hoover' up their prey from a distance, their mouths and gills sucking in powerfully. Then their heavy tooth plates crush the meal so it is ready to be swallowed. They also dig about with their powerful mouths to make shelters under rocks, jetting sand out through their gills.

Darting among the reef are clownfish which enjoy the protection of sea anemone tentacles, and are unharmed by the stinging cells. In return they protect their hosts from would-be predators. Rocks and crevices are the haunt of moray eels with their smooth, thick, scaleless skin and ferocious sharp teeth to seize and hold prey. Other predators here include sharks. The massive whale shark *(Rhincodon typus)* can measure 60ft (18m) long but is a harmless giant that eats only krill. The tiger *(Galeocerdo cuvier)* and hammerhead sharks (*Sphyrna* species), on the other hand, are potentially dangerous.

The vast manta ray *(Manta birostris)* is a plankton-eating relative of the shark – an amazing creature with forward-facing feeding lobes that filter the plankton as it glides gracefully along, its huge 'wings' rippling and casting vast purple shadows on the sea bed. These graceful swimmers can grow up to 29.5ft (9m) wide, but are usually about 22ft (6.7m) from wingtip to wingtip. On a rather smaller scale, the Red Sea is home to several types of pipefish and seahorses – enchanting little creatures that swim in a most unusual vertical mode, and wrap their curly tails around sea grass when they want to anchor down for a while. Seahorses range in size from less than half an inch (1cm) long (pygmy seahorses) to about 12in (30cm) in length.

Sahel, Niger and the Air Mountains

The word Sahel derives from the Arabic for edge or shore and is the name of a broad semi-arid belt that runs south of the Sahara Desert. This is home to many poor people who survive by herding cows, goats, and cattle, but who have little stored away to protect them against disasters, such as when the rains fail to arrive but plagues of locusts do, appearing in swarms that may be up to 43 miles (70km) long. These voracious insects devastate trees, shrubs, grasses, and hard-won crops across areas that can measure up to 4 million acres (1.6 million hectares) in the Sahel, Mali, Niger, and Senegal.

In happier times, migratory birds refuel in the Sahel and the area is home to small pale foxes *(Vulpes pallida)*, sandy-colored creatures with black-tipped tails. They scamper about, usually at night, busy in the thorny savannahs and steppes hunting insects, reptiles, or small mammals – and nibbling the odd plant or two.

Here is a landscape of sparse savannah – grasses and shrubs where the nomadic Fulani people herd their goats and cattle, and the Hausa make a brave attempt at farming. There are still camel caravans in this area, which annually collect salt from remote desert oases. The rocky outcrops of the Air Mountains rise to almost 6500ft (2000m). There are strange landscapes of blue marble, black basalt, and soaring golden dunes swept up by the prevailing winds into some of the highest sand mountains in the world. This is the land of the Tuaregs, sometimes called the 'Blue People' because of their traditional blue robes and indigo turbans and the veils that the men wear to ward off evil spirits, as well as to shield them from the harsh desert sands. They even stain their skin dark blue. Today, the Tuaregs live on the fringes of the desert, herding goats and camels, breeding cattle and transporting or selling salt.

Here, too, prehistoric man made his presence felt, creating remarkable engravings on the rocks, as well as crafting pottery, grinding stones, and fashioning flint arrowheads and stone bracelets – many of which still appear in this world of shifting sands.

Landlocked Niger borders seven other countries and is one of the hottest nations of the world (111°F, 44°C), as well as one of the poorest. Its northernmost deserts are baked mercilessly by the summer sun. The terrain of desert plains and sand dunes gives way to flatter areas and rolling plains in the south and to hills in the north. The Air Mountains receive very little annual rainfall – sometimes none at all for years on end. In the extreme south, along the edges of the River Niger, the climate is tropical. At 2600 miles (4184km) long, the Niger is the third longest river in Africa after the Nile's 4160 miles (6695km) and the Congo (Zaire) that extends 2718 miles (4374km).

Left: *Tuareg make tea at a homestead in the desert, while the camel also takes a much-needed rest. Today trains and trucks have largely replaced their caravan trade routes across the Sahara.*

Right: *A blue-robed Tuareg in Timbuktu, Mali. Traditionally Tuareg used to trade in small luxury items which could be easily transported along the caravan trade routes and which provided large profits.*

Mali

Mali is named for the Empire of Mali. This name derives from a local word for hippopotamus which features on its five-franc coin. Once upon a time, this was French Sudan. Like Niger, Mali is landlocked and has both a subtropical and an extremely arid climate – most of the country lies in the Sahara Desert. Its rolling northern plains are covered by sand, but there is savannah around the Niger River in the south and the hills in the northeast. Several ethnic groups live here as well as the nomadic Tuaregs and Maurs, who are related to the Berbers. Some 90 percent of the population of Mali follow the Sunni Islamic faith.

Above: Sankore mosque in Timbuktu has walls of mud built on a wooden framework.

Right: An oasis in North Africa. Now widely cultivated for its sweet fruit, the date palm probably originated in desert oases.

A variety of wildlife

Barbary sheep, African red deer, and two types of ibex live near the northern African coast while numerous species of antelope and deer inhabit the grassland areas. Barbary sheep *(Ammotragus lervia)* clamber nimbly through dry rocky mountain areas in the northern coastal strip, and their range extends as far east as the Red Sea and down to Northern Mali and Sudan.

The African red deer or Barbary stag *(Cervus elaphus barbarus)* is a critically endangered deer, now extinct in Morocco but still surviving in national parks near the Algerian and Tunisian frontiers, where – because of the prohibition of hunting and the reduced number of predators – the population has increased recently, even though wild boars sometimes prey on the fawns.

Several parts of Africa, including the Sudan, are home to the graceful Thomson's gazelle *(Gazella thomsoni)*, while various species of ibex live in small, protected Middle East reserves. Since Roman times ibex have been regarded as having healing powers and have been hunted almost to extinction. Today the survivors leap and scramble adeptly, usually above the tree line, but they also descend to the topmost forests to browse on buds and shoots, or to avoid the worst excesses of a harsh winter.

Over open land and semi-deserts in subSaharan Africa hovers the red kite *(Milvus milvus)* which measures about 26in (66cm) in length. The black-winged kite *(Elanus caeruleus)* is a smaller bird of prey, about 12in (31cm) in length with a white head, red eyes, and powerful beak and claws. It scans the terrain with its sharp eyes for prey such as small mammals, birds, and insects. It hunts over mangrove swamps, grasslands, and oil-palm plantations where it will find a favorite perch and then wait patiently through the hottest hours or while it is raining. Sometimes these fierce little birds fight each other in amazing aerial battles, striking upward with their talons or rolling over and locking talons, and then spinning down until perilously close to the ground.

There are several vultures in northern Africa. They scan the world below for carcasses and then make clean pickings – generally fulfilling a very useful role as they tidy up discarded left-overs. These birds can be huge and include bearded vultures *(Gypaetus barbatus)* in the high mountain areas of North Africa (whose preferred tidbits are bones) and the African white-backed vulture *(Gyps africanus)* that lives in many places south of the Sahara.

The Egyptian vulture *(Neophron percnopterus)* is predominantly a carrion eater, but also enjoys feeding on insects, fish, reptiles, and any small mammals and birds that don't make a quick enough escape. It revels in a fresh flamingo egg, and will also take a turtle up for an aerial ride and then drop it onto a rocky outcrop to smash its shell. One of the rare birds known to use tools, it will find a small stone, grip this with its beak and use it to crack open an ostrich egg, swinging its head and neck vigorously to and fro as it pounds away at the huge shell.

The griffon vulture *(Gyps fulvus)* breeds in loose colonies on crags in mountains, laying just one egg. Like other vultures, it is a scavenger, and finds food by soaring over open areas – often in flocks – its big eyes on the lookout for the tasty remains of any carrion that it can spot below.

Above: A Dogon hunter in his traditional robes. The spiritual leader of the village is the Hogon; he undergoes a six-month period of initiation, during which time he is not allowed either to shave or to wash.

Following pages: This is the largest mud structure in the world – the Grand Mosque of Djenne in Mali, first built in the 1200s by Koy Konboro, the earliest Islamic ruler. It was rebuilt in 1907. The cone-shaped spires of the mosque's three minarets are topped by ostrich egg motifs symbolizing fertility and purity.

Vultures could never be regarded as handsome, with their long scrawny necks and heads. Despite appearances to the contrary, they are not in fact bald but are covered in soft down. Having no real feathers makes poking about in carcasses a little less messy than it might otherwise be. They grunt and hiss as they feed and they also hiss when roosting.

Life in the desert

Camels and dromedaries (*Camelus bactrianus* and *Camelus dromedarius*) have been domesticated for at least 5000 years. These tough beasts can travel vast distances and survive hard times by living off the fat in their humps, which provides energy until good grazing is available again. Camels can survive on very poor vegetation during the dry summer months and are able to drink salty and brackish water. When sand storms threaten, they view the world through a third eyelid behind heavy protective eyelashes, while the hair inside their ears helps to keep the sand out – their nostrils can close too.

A camel can drink 32 gallons (120 liters) of water in just ten minutes. As well as carrying people and heavy loads through hot, inhospitable terrain, their milk can be drunk and their droppings burned as fuel. The camel can survive for up to ten days without drinking water; it conserves fluids both in body cells and in its stomach, and loses very little through perspiration, respiration, or urination. Its long legs serve to keep its body a safe distance from the hot ground – and when it does sit down, a pillow-like arrangement under its chest aids balance and provides protection from the scorching sand.

There are many cobras in Africa, including the aggressive black-necked spitting cobra *(Naja nigricollis nigricollis)* that is found from southern Egypt to northern South Africa. These rarely bite, but spit venom that can cause blindness, spraying it accurately from a distance of about 8ft (2.4m). Their colors range from dull black to pink, the lighter-colored ones being marked by a black band around the neck. Some cobras have large threatening hoods that they raise when angry or disturbed.

Asps or Egyptian cobras *(Naja haje)* are widely distributed throughout Africa, and are famous for their use by snake charmers. Not only do they look splendid but they also respond well to visual cues, weaving and dancing under the direction of their 'trainers.' This snake's powerful venom (ten times more potent than that of the Indian cobra) causes a fast, painless death.

Another snake that zig-zags its way across the hot sand is the horned desert viper *(Cerastes cerastes)*. When moving about in the heat, they usually travel by sidewinding so that their bodies shade their heads to help keep the sun out of their faces. When the heat proves too overpowering, these creatures bury themselves in the sand in order to keep cool, leaving only the head and eyes visible. They usually hunt in the cool of night but may stay half-buried even then, lunging quickly from their sandy hidey-holes to grab an unwary lizard or rodent. Sometimes the snake will scrape its scales together to make a threatening noise. The two 'horns' from which it gets its name may protect the snake's eyes from injury or perhaps serve as a form of camouflage.

Above and following pages: Egypt's largest camel market in Birqash, on the edge of the Western Desert near Cairo. Most of the camels are brought on foot from Sudan along the Forty Days Road.

Opposite: The sun casts long shadows as a camel caravan crosses the inhospitable Sahara. Camels are able to survive for about ten days without water.

Scorpions are predominately found in tropical or subtropical climates and were probably among the first predators to walk the Earth. Scorpions have been hunting, stinging, and killing their victims for some 420 million years and appeared on Earth long before the dinosaurs. Some 30 species of these nocturnal creatures are venomous but although scorpion bites are excruciatingly painful, they are not usually deadly to humans, although the aggressive fat-tailed scorpion *(Androctonus australis)* is responsible for numerous deaths each year in North Africa. Scorpions live in many different habitats, including rainforests, deserts, plains and savannahs, mountainous pine forests, and caves. They survive in the remotest parts of the Sahara and hibernate in snowy zones. Often, scorpions will ambush their prey, lying in wait as they sense its approach. Smaller ones eat insects, spiders, centipedes – and even other scorpions. The diet of larger scorpions may include small lizards, snakes, and mice. Young scorpions are born alive and then climb onto their mothers' backs to be carried safely under her sting for a couple of weeks until their first molt, after which they are big and fierce enough to face the world alone.

The pretty little fennec fox *(Vulpes zerda)* is one of the most attractive desert mammals, a solitary creature that lives in burrows in arid regions of North Africa. Their enormous ears help them to listen out for prey – and enemies – and act as cooling mechanisms to get rid of excess heat. Fennec foxes are primarily

Above: *The small fennec fox has enormous ears. Its feet have furred soles so that it can cross the hot desert sand in comfort.*

Right: *This is the Sahara, the largest desert in the world, sweeping through 11 countries. In places, the wind creates high mountains of sand which flow in ever-changing shapes and ripple patterns.*

nocturnal, their large, dark eyes providing good night vision as they pad quietly across the sand. When threatened, they can leap nearly four times their body length from a standing position. They also spring off the ground when hunting – to land with their front feet on their prey.

The opportunistic golden jackal *(Canis aureus)* is widely distributed across north and east Africa. It generally lives in dry, open grassland with trees and brush but is also found in desert areas, oases, and at high altitudes. This is the only jackal that ranges across northern Africa and it was the inspiration for the Ancient Egyptian deity Anubis, the god of death who assisted at the passage to the next life. This figure is widely depicted in Egyptian temples and tombs. Golden jackals eat plants and fruit, as well as rabbits, rodents, birds, eggs, grasshoppers, insects, frogs, snakes, fish, and carrion. They also steal food from larger predators. The distinctive howl of this jackal can be heard for miles.

Several sorts of gerbil hail from Africa. These scampering little rodents measure from 3-7in (7-18cm) long with tails of 3-9in (7-23cm) and were once called 'desert rats'. The family includes over 100 species, including sand rats and jirds, all living happily in arid desert habitats. Most are primarily nocturnal. The fat-tailed gerbil *(Pachyuromys duprasi)* lives in the Sahara, and its very short tail gets ever plumper around the tip. Naked-sole gerbils (*Tatera* sp. are large and *Taterillus* sp. very small) have no hair on the bottom of their feet. Jirds live in North Africa, in Libya and Morocco for instance. They are skilled acrobats and can jump high like a tiny kangaroo to avoid capture by a hungry predator.

The common gecko originated in North Africa but has now spread around the world – some having been carried unwittingly on ships to destinations as diverse as southern France, the Canary Islands, and South Pacific islands. These appealing lizards are now often kept as pets. Even when living in the wild, they often move into houses to feed on insect pests. They make chirping sounds and can climb smooth vertical surfaces or cross ceilings with ease, thanks to their adhesive, flattened toe pads. Geckos have small, plump bodies and large heads and eyes. Many are vividly colored, and some even change color. They live in a wide range of habitats including tropical rainforests, deserts, icy mountain peaks – and human houses. Most geckos hunt at night, enjoying a supper of beetles, butterflies, millipedes, crickets, and cockroaches. If threatened, geckos can shed their tail; a new shorter one grows in its place. Sometimes the old one fails to break off completely and the creature may end up with two, or even three, tails.

Bats and birds

The larger fruit bats live only in tropical areas of Africa, usually in huge colonies in dense forests. Their big eyes enable them to orient themselves in the twilight and their sense of smell is excellent. The Egyptian fruit bat *(Rousettus aegyptiacus)* uses high-pitched clicks as an echo-location device to navigate in dark caves, where they sleep crowded together to keep warm. Other fruit bats sleep in trees. These flying mammals have wings that look like long fingers covered by a thin skin membrane. They are superb at flying and hanging upside down, but cannot walk well on their weak legs. Fruit bats eat fruits or suck nectar from flowers,

inserting their long tongues deep inside the bloom. They chew the juicy fruit, then spit out seeds, peel and pulp – in this way helping to disperse the seeds.

The little egret *(Egretta garzetta)* and cattle egret *(Bubulcus ibis)* breed in colonies in trees close to large lakes with reed beds or other wetlands, such as the Nile. They feed in shallow water, often waiting silently and motionless for prey to appear, or slowly stalking a fish, frog, or insect before spearing their victim with a long, sharp bill.

White pelicans *(Pelecanus onocrotalus)* occur throughout Africa on large areas of inland water. Some migrate but sedentary populations are found all year round south of the Sahara Desert. They inhabit lakes, rivers, coastlines, and estuaries, where the breeding colony may number up to 60,000 birds. The pelican has a spectacularly large bill and a bright yellow, elastic pouch that can hold an enormous volume of fish. Usually they fish as a group, carefully herding the fish into shallow water where they can easily be caught and slid into the bird's huge throat pouch. This is just temporary storage, for the main purpose of the pouch is to act as a kind of fishing net. The pelican will then tilt its bill up and swallow the fish whole. White pelicans are surface feeders and do not dive for fish.

Previous pages: The bearded vulture is so called because of the long tufts of feathers near its beak. It eats bones, breaking larger ones by dropping them from a height onto rocky outcrops and devouring both the marrow and the bone splinters themselves.

Opposite: Ghost crabs scuttle along quickly, changing direction to confuse predators as they cross the sand and then disappear into tunnels burrowed down some 4ft (over 1m) under the surface.

Below: A papyrus plant provides a perch for the attractive pied kingfisher, ever on the lookout for fish or crustaceans to eat.

The pied kingfisher *(Ceryle rudis)* is widespread across Africa and this pretty little black-and-white crested bird can often be seen hovering above the surface of water – and not necessarily just a riverbank. It will fish way out on an open lake or beyond coastal breakers. They gather in family groups, often roosting in papyrus beds and nesting in burrows, with the previous season's offspring generally helping to raise the next brood. These elegant birds survey their hunting ground, either hovering high over open water or watching from an advantageous perch. While relatively small at 10in (25cm) long, this is the largest bird that can hover in still air.

There are lots of ghost crabs in South Africa, Equatorial Guinea, and along the Red Sea coast. These busy little creatures scuttle over the sand and spend a large part of their waking hours between dusk and dawn burrowing to make new 'dens,' so leaving the beach liberally sprinkled with holes. They can be both carnivorous and cannibalistic and their sharp black eyes have 360-degree lateral vision which helps them to catch flying insects in mid-air. Looking directly up, however, is not part of the package so the crab must burrow into the ground to hide from predatory birds. Their green-gray shell and claws become pale white if exposed to white sand in full sunlight – hence their name.

Conclusion

So this is where Africa begins, where the 'dark continent' is anything but dark, as snowflakes tumble on the Atlas Mountains while the fierce sun blazes down on the Sahara Desert. Its sharp contrasts introduce the African dream, encapsulating the spirit of the very different world that lies south of the Mediterranean.

Above: *The cattle egret is often found beside large mammals, enjoying the insects they disturb. If the birds spot a distant fire, they will fly toward it to catch insects trying to escape the flames.*

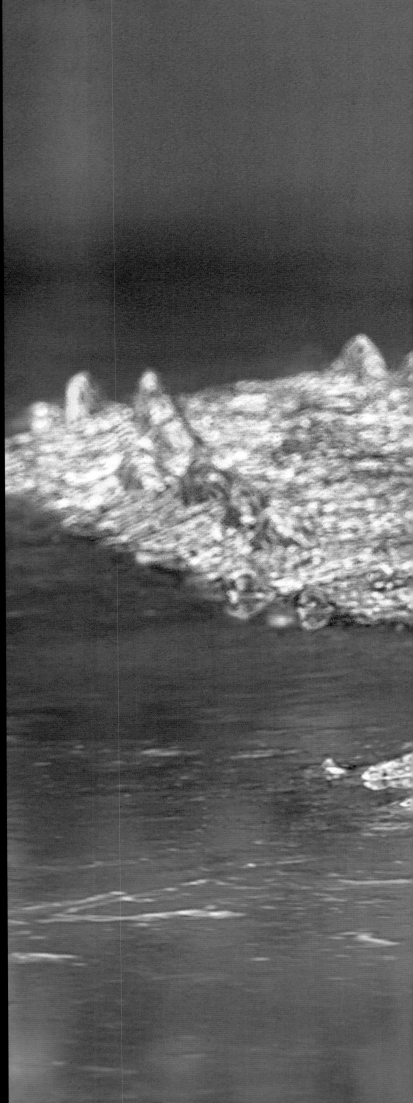

Previous pages: Chott El Djerid, Tunisia, is a vast salt 'lake' that measures some 1900sq miles (4920km²) in area but now is almost completely dried out. Winter rainfall drains into the salt lakes and then evaporates, leaving behind a thick salt crust.

Above: An ibex, a large mountain goat with scimitar-like horns, scrambles nimbly through North Africa's rocky terrain.

Right: Nile crocodiles occupy many of Africa's lakes, rivers, and swamps. They may sunbathe on a bank to warm up early in the day but thereafter they often remain semi-submerged in water, keeping cool but watchful.

Above: *A horned viper winds its way across the hot desert. Soon it will bury itself in the sand to keep cool before emerging again at night to hunt for lizards and rodents.*
Left: *A satellite photograph taken in low Earth orbit shows the Sahel region and the fertile inland delta of the Niger River, sprinkled with a scattering of clouds.*

Following pages: *A pirogue (dug-out canoe) at sunset on the delta of the River Niger – the third longest river in Africa. It flows for 2600 miles (4184km) through Mali, Niger, and Nigeria to the Gulf of Guinea.*

WEST AFRICA

Here lies one-fifth of Africa, an area that encompasses low plains, semi-arid terrain, and savannah to the south of the Sahara Desert and lush equatorial forests that create a green strip between savannah and coast. The River Niger rises in Guinea and flows some 2600 miles (4814km) through Mali, Niger, and Nigeria. There are patches of damp forest all along the coast, as well as mangrove swamps and dry semi-deciduous forests just a little farther inland – each with its own distinctive blend of flora and fauna.

Mary Kingsley, a Victorian traveler and collector of specimens for the British Museum, was passionate about West Africa. Describing her adventures in a lecture at Cheltenham Ladies College, England, she recalled: '*Once a hippopotamus and I were on an island together, and I wanted one of us to leave. I preferred it should be myself, but the hippo was close to my canoe, and looked like staying, so I made cautious and timorous advances to him and finally scratched him behind the ear with my umbrella and we parted on good terms. But with the crocodile it was different.*'

A vast range of flora and fauna flourish in this region, especially in the tropical forest habitats but also in places like Mount Cameroon where over 2500 plant species have been recorded. Ebony, iroko, and mahogany come from this part of the world, as do rubber plants and the oil palm. Mangrove forests straddle sandy beaches, creating an amazingly rich habitat for marine life and roosts for coastal birds. They are now also seen as a good natural defense against tsunamis.

People and culture

This region is home to many ethnic peoples whose religions include Islam (especially in the West African interior and far west coast) and Christianity in the coastal regions of Nigeria, Ghana, and the Côte d'Ivoire. This is also the home of voodoo, an ancient, mysterious and much maligned religion practiced by some 30 million people in the West African nations of Benin, Togo, and Ghana.

The Bobo, Faso, and Fon

The Bobo have lived for centuries in western Burkina on the southern fringes of the Sahara Desert where wide flat plains meet hills in the west and far southeast, and the Black, Red, and White Volta rivers flow south into Ghana. Predominantly farmers and cotton traders, they wear masks and elaborate outfits for celebrations. Meanwhile, the Faso have also managed to retain their own culture despite successive Islamic invasions. They live in Burkina Faso, a landlocked nation surrounded by Mali, Niger, Benin, Togo, Ghana, and the Côte d'Ivoire.

Some two million Fon live in Benin and Nigeria. This culture permits divorce and polygamy and celebrates death with elaborate mourning rituals – people dance and play drums for many days. Because the slave trade transported so many people from western Africa across the Atlantic, many Fon also live in the Americas now.

The Hausa-Fulani

The Fulani are the largest nomadic group in the world, and are widespread in many parts of West Africa, with a history that stretches back over a thousand years. Once herders and traders who established numerous trade routes and were responsible for introducing and spreading Islam throughout much of western Africa, they conquered and absorbed a large number of people from diverse groups. The Hausa city-states were probably founded between the late 900s and early 1200s while the Fulani empire was dominant through the 1800s and early 1900s. Hausa is the most commonly used language in West Africa, spoken by about 25 million people. Cattle are of prime importance in their culture, influencing names, traditions, and taboos – with the number owned being an indication of wealth. Their strict caste system divides people into nobility, merchants, blacksmiths, and slave descendants.

Most Hausa live in small villages, growing crops and raising livestock. Cotton grew readily on the great plains of these states, and these people became the primary producers, weaving and dying the cloth before sending it to market in caravans. Beautiful indigo dyed cloth is still produced in northern Nigeria. These people are also skilled horse riders and musicians.

The Mandinka

The Mandinka is an ethnic group that populates Senegal, Gambia, Guinea-Bissau, plus Burkina Faso, Mali, and Côte d'Ivoire. Their rich culture incorporates music, especially drumming and the kora – a 21-string 'harp-lute' made out of a gourd covered with cow skin, and with fishing line strings. The Mandinka have infused Islam with their own culture. So while they may pray to Allah five times a day, they may also make sacrifices to a village god or spirit. Rural subsistence farmers grow peanuts, rice, millet and keep goats for their livelihood.

The Slave Trade

Slaves had been bought and sold along the trans-Saharan trade route since pre-Roman times but the trade accelerated as Islam spread in the 700s – every year from around AD 800 to the 1600s, between 5000 and 10,000 slaves were exported from Africa. When, from the 1480s, gold lured the Europeans into West Africa they capitalized on the existing slave trade, and from 1485 to 1540 some 12,000 slaves were imported by the Portuguese and sold to gold merchants from places as far away as Mali.

As the European presence in West Africa increased, the trade in gold, ivory, and pepper escalated, as did the slave trade. The Portuguese used slaves to work in gold mines and sugar plantations while prisoners of war from local inter-tribal disputes – and criminals – were sold to the Europeans in exchange for firearms that could then be used to capture even more tribesmen. Soon this human cargo became a major source of income – and dispute – as rival Dutch, Portuguese, Scottish, Swedish, Danish, and English companies struggled for supremacy along the coast where the slave ships waited for their cargoes of captives, who were marched there to be held in 'slave castles' along the coast.

Page 58: Senegal street vendors sell fruit in front of striking ocher-painted buildings.
Page 59: Ghana: waves on Accra beach reflect the gold of the sunset.

Left: A view from the tower of Ghana's Fort St. Jago, where slaves and gold were traded.
Above: A young Hausa girl in a traditional blue headdress.

Opposite: A smiling Gambian woman from Albreda village with braided hair and wearing a traditional headdress.

Above left and top: A voodoo priest stands by a painted wall while the interior of the voodoo temple houses a strange assembly of

Above: A pile of rather gruesome-looking voodoo items – the dried heads of a variety of wild animals – are offered for sale in a

As many as 15 to 20 million people may have been enslaved – but many died on the march to the coast, and in the cellars of slave forts such as Cape Coast Castle on Ghana's shores where 1000 male and 500 female slaves were locked into dank dungeons for six to 12 weeks at a time, waiting for the slave ships to dock. Another 25-50 percent of those crammed like sardines into the slave ships would die before reaching the Americas. Many were taken to the West Indies, chained at the wrists and legs with irons, or packed tightly into the lower decks.

Estimates of the numbers transported vary from 12 million to 25 million; in 1700, at the height of the trade, over 650,000 slaves may have been exported in that one year alone – mostly from West Africa and the Congo-Angola region. Britain abolished its slave trade in 1807, but the trade did not finally die out until the 1870s.

Senegal

Senegal lies on the edge of Africa's bulbous northwestern region, bounded by the Atlantic Ocean, with its capital, Dakar, the most westerly point of the continent. Slaves, ivory, and gold were exported from the coast during the 1600s and 1700s but now the economy is based on agriculture. With semi-desert in the north and northeast, and a moist, tropical south with forests, the country surrounds the Gambia on three sides. It is low-lying, with its largest rivers the Senegal in the north and the Casamance in the south. It is home to the Wolof people, who traditionally lived in small villages, governed by extended family units, but many of whom now work in cities. There are also some Fulani and Serer in the south and some sources suggest that the people came originally from Ancient Egypt.

In this area elephants, mongooses, antelope, buffalo, bushbuck, waterbuck, hartebeest, and pairs of little dik dik are found. Monkeys and a wide variety of birds live in the dense forests while crocodile and hippopotamus abound in lakes and rivers.

African clawless otters *(Aonyx capensis)* live in rivers in savannah and lowland forested areas from Senegal to Ethiopia and south to the Cape. They are happiest where the current is slow-moving, and where loops in the rivers create pools. They have soft, velvety fur and feet that look like little hands – with five fingers, no webbing or claws, but tiny growths like fingernails. Their large strong teeth can crack open mollusk shells and they also eat turtles, fish, frogs, lizards, aquatic birds, and small mammals. They generally capture prey in their paws, using their bright eyes to spot a tasty morsel or, in murkier waters, relying on their long sensitive whiskers. Sometimes they knead the mud to find worms.

A baby crested porcupine *(Hystrix cristata)* stays in the nest for about two weeks until its newborn soft spines have hardened and it is ready to bristle its way out into the world. Their tails have special hollow quills that can rattle a warning at potential predators.

Vervet monkeys *(Cercopithecus aethiops)* are found in the trees in many parts of Africa, but especially in acacia woodlands alongside streams, rivers, and lakes in this part of the continent. They sleep and eat in the safety of the trees, rarely scurrying farther than a few hundred yards away from them for fear of the

leopards, cheetahs, caracal, baboons, large eagles, crocodiles, and pythons that might snap them up as food. Troops of these greenish-olive or silvery-gray monkeys can number from five up to 20 or more, and they spend many hours sitting in the trees grooming and removing parasites and other bits and pieces of debris from one another's fur.

The Gambia

The Gambia is the smallest country on mainland Africa, with colorful Banjul its capital. This sliver of land runs along both sides of the meandering Gambia River and has become a popular tourist destination with its pleasant subtropical climate. It has two distinct seasons – dry from November to June when the savannah winds blow and there is virtually uninterrupted glorious sunshine and clear blue skies; and wet from July to October with heavy showers when the country turns lusciously green. The Gambia is home to the Mandinka tribe, as well as Fula, Wolof, Jola, and Serahule peoples.

Here ants, chameleons, and lizards (including geckos and monitors) scuttle among the trees and undergrowth. There are many squirrels (gray, striped ground, and sun squirrels) while the air is busy with butterflies, dragonflies and some 500 species of birds, including frigates, heron, spoonbill, flamingo, stork, vultures, eagles, buzzards, and kites.

Fiddler crabs can be seen permanently bustling about on the shores, mangrove swamps, and tidal creeks – feeding, fighting, mating, cleaning up their burrow sites, or waving their claws. Only the male boasts the outrageously enormous single claw that is used for display during courtship, for warning off intruders, and for signaling to each other. They may lose this weapon during a fight but a new one will grow – albeit a smaller version.

Monkeys found here include the red colobus *(Procolobus badius)* and the patas monkey *(Erythrocebus patas)*. This little creature is a veritable Olympic champion of the animal world and holds the monkey speed-record, reaching over 31mph (50km/h) in about three seconds on its long, strong legs and short feet and toes. Despite the threats of predators, the speedy patas are able to survive at ground level especially in areas of acacia bushes where trees are few.

Equatorial Guinea

The North Atlantic Ocean pounds the beaches of Equatorial Guinea. It enjoys a tropical climate so is hot and humid all year round and sometimes buffeted by severe windstorms. An average of some 181in (4600mm) of rain falls each year. Thickly forested hills slope down to meet the coastal plains and beyond these lie the Gulf of Guinea (or Cameroon Line) Islands – a group of exposed volcanic peaks consisting of Annobon, São Tomé, Principe, and Bioko. Mount Cameroon

Previous pages: An initiation ceremony takes place in a Senegal village. Boys dance around a thatched hut inside which other young men await the initiation rite.

Right: A beach fish market in the Gambia. This small narrow country straddles both banks of the meandering Gambia River and the main crop grown is peanuts.

Top: Pelicans splash down on the water at high speed when they land.

Above: The hands of a clawless otter are similar to those of a monkey; it uses them to catch octopus, frogs, crabs, and crayfish. The otter's sleek body and waterproof coat help it to glide smoothly through the water.

Right: Vervet monkeys are found from the southern Sahara to the Cape, living in troops of between 10 and 50 individuals. Vulnerable to attacks by leopards and other predatory cats, baboons, eagles, crocodiles, and pythons, they remain in the safety of the trees for most of the time.

which lies in Cameroon is part of this geological range. It reaches 13,435ft (4095m) and is the highest point in West Africa. The island of Bioko (where the nation's capital, Malabo, is situated) is actually three extinct volcanoes – one of which reaches 9875ft (3010m). The country supports many temperate plants and animals. There are forests of okume, mahogany, and walnut trees while cocoa, coffee, cassava, sweet potatoes, bananas, palm oil, and palm kernels are cultivated on the fertile volcanic soil.

Most of the inhabitants speak a Bantu language. The main ethnic group is the Fang which is of Bantu origin – most other groups have been pushed to the coast by Fang expansion. The Bubi are the indigenous ethnic group of Bioko Island and are descendants of slaves (liberated by the British in the 1800s) and Nigerians and Fangs who migrated here in the 1900s.

Bioko is a continental shelf island, separated by rising sea levels from mainland Africa after the last Ice Age c.10,000 years ago. Because of this isolation, the island boasts several unique species and has become a valued 'hotspot' for primate conservation. Its seven species of monkeys include black and red colobus and various guenons including the red-eared, crowned, and Martin's putty-nosed guenon – all agile, vocal monkeys.

There are also duiker (forest antelope), genet, civet, tree hyrax, brush-tailed porcupine, giant pouched rat – and the African giant squirrel (*Protoxerus stangeri*) that stays safely up in the high tree canopy.

Mandrills live in many of the dense rainforests of Africa (species here include *Mandrillus leucophaeus poensis* and *Mandrillus sphinx*). The brightly colored males have red noses and lips, white ears, white lines with purple stripes on their faces, and yellow manes and beards. They also have bright purple rumps, and are very spectacular beasts. They live in big troops of 100 or more, and forage for seeds, nuts, and fruits, stuffing these in their large cheek pouches to eat later in a safer location.

Named for this part of the world, the helmeted guineafowl (*Numida meleagris*) is a chicken-like bird with a horny growth on the head, white-spotted feathers, and fleshy cheek wattles. From its ancestors, the domestic guineafowl descended. These gregarious ground-feeders eat seeds, berries, leaves, insects, snails, and spiders. They can run some 3 miles (5km) in a day and make loud harsh calls if disturbed. At night, these noisy birds settle at last to roost in the trees.

Sierra Leone

The literal meaning of Sierra Leone is 'Lion Mountains' and there are indeed mountains here in the northeast of the country. The highest point is Loma Mansa, at 6391ft (1948m). The coastline consists mainly of mangrove swamps, except for the peninsula upon which the capital city, Freetown, is situated. The rest is mostly forest-covered plateau with a typical tropical climate – the rain pours down from May to December. This is a poor country with the lowest average income in the world.

One of the most important tribes is the Temne (found mostly in the north), who developed the kola nut trade during the days of the Mali and Songhai

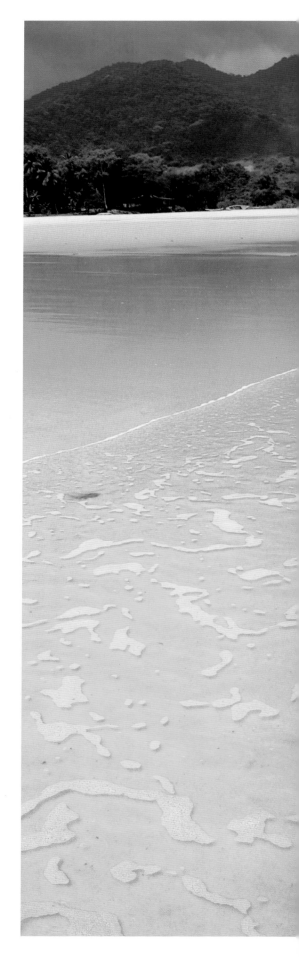

empires in the 15th and 16th centuries when West African trade extended north across the Sahara Desert. The name of the drink Coca-Cola probably derived from this nut's name. Today the Temne are mainly farmers, coastal fishermen, and traders. The Mende – now primarily in the south and east – migrated here from western Sudan. During the centuries of slavery, many were shipped to Cuba but the descendants of those that escaped this fate now grow crops like rice or are traders. Exports include diamonds, cocoa, coffee, and fish.

Wild dogs, elephants, lions, duiker (Zebra and Jentink's), and spotted-necked otters are found in this part of Africa – as are troops of the rare western red colobus *(Procolobus badius)* leaping through the foliage, swinging on their long limbs, and using the elasticity of a branch to catapult themselves between trees. They feed mainly on flowers, leaves, and shoots.

Western chimpanzees *(Pan troglodytes)* survive in areas of Guinea and Sierra Leone. They are supposed to be protected in most places but are still illegally hunted to eat or to sell, while the diminishing forest habitat has also reduced their numbers. Once common in the African forest belt that stretched across from Senegal to Tanzania, now fewer than 300,000 survive. These intelligent primates use tools and young chimps learn how to make them by watching others. They employ sticks to extract termites from earth mounds to eat and crumple up leaves to soak up water to drink. They also treat illnesses and injuries with medicinal plants. Mother chimpanzees may develop lifelong relationships

Left: *Atlantic waves sweep across the golden sands of Mama Beach near Tembo in Sierra Leone.*

Above: *Western chimpanzees use many facial expressions, sounds, and gestures to communicate to one another.*

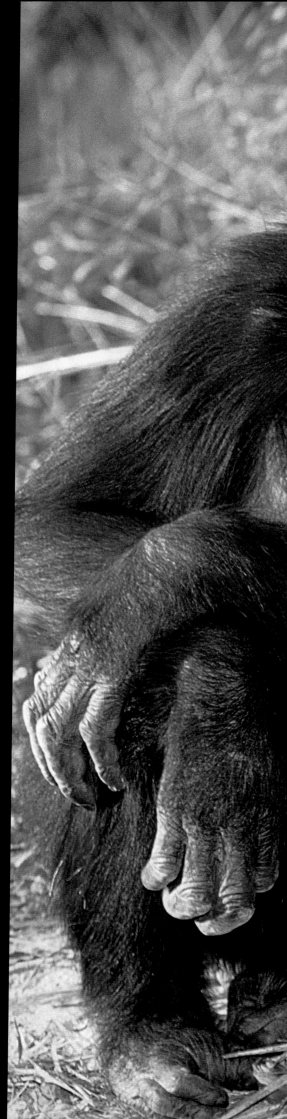

Above: *Sierra Leone's Freetown was founded in 1787 as a place of refuge for liberated slaves. Nearby is beautiful Bureh Beach, its sands and forested hinterland sliced in two by a river.*

Right: *Chimpanzees are highly intelligent primates that inhabit western and central Africa. They learn quickly, use tools, can accomplish complex tasks and, each evening, create individual 'sleeping nests' in the trees. Sadly, increasing deforestation has made them an endangered species.*

with their offspring and all of them are very social, communicating vocally as well as with facial expressions, body language, mutual grooming, and affectionate kisses and pats.

The beautiful Diana monkey *(Cercopithecus diana)* is found in ancient forests in West Africa from Sierra Leone to Ghana. They are named for the ancient Roman goddess Diana: the white stripe across their foreheads resembles her bow. In a quite ungodlike manner, when in danger or competing for the best pickings, they pack their cheek pouches with a stomach's load of food and then find a more secure location to enjoy this feast. They have a wide range of alarm calls which are specific to particular predators.

Twice the size of a domestic cat, the African golden cat *(Profelis aurata)* can be chestnut red or silver, spotted or plain. This is a solitary hunter that stalks small antelope, rodents, tree hyraxes, and birds in the tropical rainforest of equatorial Africa.

Côte d'Ivoire

The Republic of the Côte d'Ivoire (formerly called the Ivory Coast) lies on the south coast of the western bulge of Africa. The peaks of the Guinea Highlands in the northwest rise to 5000ft (1525m), but most of the region is a vast gently sloping plateau that is crossed by four major rivers: the Cavally, Sassandra, Bandama Blanc, and Komoé. All are sluggish in the dry season but busy with falls and rapids – and liable to flood – when the rains arrive. The lagoon region is a narrow coastal belt dotted with low, sandy islands and sandbars created by the mix of heavy surf and ocean currents. Dense mangrove thickets edge narrow, salty inlets, these fingers of marsh pointing inward to a broad belt of dense forest that covers nearly one-third of the country. The northern half is mostly savannah grassland – a large plateau with rolling hills, scrubby vegetation, and scattered trees.

The Dan people who live here are renowned as excellent farmers. Many moved south to Mali and Côte d'Ivoire in 1400s and 1500s. Portuguese trading ships arrived in the 1460s. Later, in the 1840s, France persuaded local chiefs to grant their traders a monopoly along the coast here, and then established naval bases to keep out others. This done, they set about conquering the interior, fighting the Mandinka forces from Gambia in the 1890s and repulsing other guerrilla attacks.

Coffee, cocoa, and palm oil crops were soon planted along the coast, and tended by local forced labor under the control of French settlers. Today the Côte d'Ivoire is one of the world's main cocoa producers, supplying some 41 percent of the global market.

Over 1200 animal species are found here (232 mammals, 702 birds, 125 reptiles, 38 amphibians, 111 fish) as well as 4700 plant species. The rugged interior is especially rich in wildlife and over 4300sq miles (11,000km²) of the Parc National de la Comoé is home to lions, elephants, hippos, and countless birds.

The rare purple-brown pygmy hippopotamus *(Choeropsis liberiensis)* has a barrel-shaped body about 4 to 6ft (1.2-1.9m) long (ordinary Nile hippos can be over 13ft/4m in length). It has pinkish cheeks and a shiny moist hide. While

Above: *The red-billed hornbill is nimble enough to catch swarming termites in flight and chases grasshoppers along the ground to eat.*
Opposite: *A pygmy hippopotamus wallows happily in mud. They live in rivers and swamps in dense forests in western Africa, and are more pig-shaped than their larger Nile relatives.*

trundling about close to water (into which it may dive if frightened), this creature spends more time on land than its larger relative and so has longer legs (for its size) and minimal webbing between its four toes. Its stubby little tail sports a tassel of yellow hair.

West African manatees *(Trichechus senegalensis)* are large, cylindrically-shaped aquatic mammals with whiskery snouts, flexible flippers, and back ends that look like rounded, horizontal paddles. They use their flippers to propel their heavy bodies along the bottom of the waters in which they live, to manipulate food and also to scratch, touch, and even embrace other manatees. The West African manatee lives in coastal areas, estuary lagoons, large rivers, and freshwater lakes. Some feed exclusively on mangroves. The molar teeth with which they crush vegetation grow continuously at the back of the jaw and move forward as the older ones wear down and drop out. Together with their close relatives, the dugong, these are the only plant-eating marine mammals. The West African is unfortunately the most threatened of the manatee species.

Ghana

The north of the interior of neighboring Ghana comprises low bush, savannah, and grassy plains set beyond a lush green strip of tropical rainforest where heavily forested hills rise above the jungle and streams and rivers gleam like silver threads in between. All this is edged by a sandy coastline.

Once the site of a number of ancient kingdoms, and then coming under British colonial rule, this was the first subSaharan African country to obtain its independence in 1957. The Anlo-Ewe people had settled in the southeastern corner in about 1474, but some 500 years later the Ashanti became a major ethnic group in central Ghana. This was another area where slavery was an important trade. During the 1600s and 1700s about 60 forts and trading posts appeared along Ghana's 335-mile (540km) stretch of coast. The dramatic Cape Coast Castle was the capital of the British slave trade in west Africa for more than a century during which some 100,000 people a year were dragged there before being transported across the Atlantic.

Today skilled local weavers still make the wonderfully colorful Kente cloth that they have been creating since the 1100s, with major weaving centers found near the city of Kumasi. The long strips of cloth are sewn together to create generous wraps, much favored by Ghanaian chiefs and also purchased by tourists. They are highly valued for their richness and symbolism – each woven motif has a special meaning pertinent to their culture.

Ghana is home to nearly 250 species of mammals which include black and white colobus, chimpanzees, Diana monkeys, elephants, and hippos, while bird populations include gray- and red-fronted parrots and the red-necked buzzard.

There are bushbabies in many parts of Africa (the only continent on which they are found) including Ghana and Senegal. Nine species include the greater bushbaby *(Otolemur crassicaudatus)* and the lesser bushbaby or Senegal galago *(Galago senegalensis)*. They live in the trees in savannah, bush, and forest, their huge staring eyes affording these nocturnal creatures magnificent night vision.

Previous page: This traditional, flat-roofed mud house in Sirigu, Ghana, has brightly painted walls featuring symbolic geometric patterns. Sirigu is widely celebrated for the quality of its expressive wall decorations and its attractive local pottery.

Above: Fortifications at Cape Coast Castle, Ghana, where slaves were once traded.
Right: Ghana has 335 miles (540km) of coastline. These fishermen are in Elmina harbor below St George's Castle. This fort was founded in 1482 by the Portuguese and visited by Christopher Columbus 10 years prior to his first voyage to the Americas.

They have fluffy fur, small pointed faces, and naked, highly mobile ears. These appealing little animals are swift and agile, leaping like squirrels from branch to branch or hopping across the ground. Their call is like the cry of a baby – hence their name.

The honey badger or ratel *(Mellivora capensis)* is a tenacious and brave little carnivore, described in the 2002 *Guinness Book of Records* as the most fearless animal in the world. These secretive creatures enjoy a diet of beetles, scorpions, lizards, rodents, birds, polecats, young foxes, and jackals, and they will even tackle larger creatures, such as antelope, wild cats, small crocodiles, and pythons, and poisonous snakes, such as cobras and black mambas. They climb up into the highest branches of trees to raid bird nests and beehives. They relish the sweet honey but also love munching the bee brood and the larvae of solitary bees.

Forest hogs

The giant forest hog *(Hylochoerus meinertzhageni)*, as its name indicates, is a vast dark brown or black hairy boar up to 6.5ft (2m) in length. They trot through the tropical forests, usually at night, and live in herds of up to about 20, except when breeding when pairs become intolerant of others. The females build a nest of bamboo stalks and, once the young are on the move, the babies feed from any lactating female and are protected by all of them. These fierce hogs have a short mane that rises when they are excited.

Warthogs *(Phacochoerus aethiopicus* and *Phacochoerus africanus)* live in the open, dry steppes and savannahs south of the Sahara. They are the only pigs that (like camels and some gazelles) can survive in places that see no rainfall for several months of the year. The name warthog refers to the large warts on their faces but, somehow, their ugliness is appealing. Eyes set up high allow them to spot predators even when their heads and snouts are munching short grass. They scamper along with their tails upright, the little bristly tufts at the end waving like flags, perhaps helping young ones to keep together in single file.

Left: *Warthogs live in the savannah and enjoy wallowing in mud. They also take sand baths, rub against trees and termite mounds, and let tick birds prise off any parasites. They have poor vision but a good sense of smell and hearing. An alarmed warthog will flatten its ears, snort or grunt, lower its mane, and then scamper to safety.*

Right: *This mosque in Larabanga, Ghana, is one of the oldest in West Africa. Constructed from mud, it houses an ancient copy of the Koran which is brought out only once a year at a special ceremony.*

Above: Brilliantly patterned Kente cloth. The different patterns woven into the fabric embody traditional concepts and symbols.

Opposite: A stern, dignified Hausa chief from Niger. The earliest Hausa leaders claim descent from their founder, Bayajidda. Later rulers adopted the Islamic faith but still honored long-standing Hausa traditions.

Specialist behavior

Cattle egrets *(Bubulcus ibis)* eat insects such as locusts and grasshoppers, small crustaceans, frogs, tadpoles, mollusks, fish, lizards, and small birds. They roost and nests in large colonies in trees and often frequent damp pastures near cows and buffalo, on the watch for any grasshoppers or beetles disturbed by the grazing beasts. Sometimes they perch on the back of a cow, looking for ticks and flies. They can catch and eat over 100 an hour, so the cattle welcome their attentions which rid them of troublesome pests.

Africa has many kinds of mongoose living in its savannahs, woodlands, grasslands, and semi-arid bush. These include the white-tailed *(Ichneumia albicauda)* and dwarf mongoose *(Helogale parvula)* and the dark brown marsh mongoose *(Atilax paludinosus)* which is found in Ghana and all the wetter parts of Africa. It eats fruit but its sharp, strong teeth can kill and devour small animals too. It will bash an awkward crab or bird's egg against a stone to smash it open. This wily creature will also lie on its back, flaunting its pale pink bottom like a lure. When a bird swoops down to investigate, the mongoose grabs yet another tasty meal!

Nigeria

This, the most populous country in Africa, has been inhabited since about 9000 BC and was the first home of the Bantu. Today Nigeria can lay claim to more than 250 ethnic groups with a rich diversity of languages and customs. The largest is the Ibo and numerous extended families live in villages. The Yoruba, who inhabit southwest Nigeria and Benin, are renowned for their pottery, weaving, beadwork, metalwork, and mask making. Today the capital city is Abuja, which replaced Lagos in this capacity in 1991.

There are many different habitats in Nigeria. In the south, a 500-mile (800km) stretch of sandy beaches is backed by mangrove swamps and lagoons. Behind this, lowlands and then a broad hilly region rise, and farther inland are dense tropical rainforests. In the north lie hills and the great plateau of Nigeria, where plains and savannah merge into scrubland. The Adamawa Massif (which continues into Cameroon) boasts Nigeria's highest point, Mt Vogel, at 6700ft (2042m) with the Sahel and Sahara desert stretching beyond. The lower course of the Niger River flows south through the western part of the country into the Gulf of Guinea.

Nigeria's diverse habitat supports an equally diverse range of plants and animals. The world's largest variety of butterflies are found in this country while wild drill monkeys only occur in southeast Nigeria and neighboring Cameroon.

Sadly in recent decades, rapid population growth and spreading farmlands have swallowed up huge areas of wild habitat while the hunting of animals for food has also threatened their survival. Now Nigeria's elephants, buffalo, lions, leopards and other large game are generally found only in very remote areas or in game reserves. Smaller animals, such as antelope, monkeys, jackals, and hyenas, do remain common, however, while hippopotamuses and crocodiles still haunt the larger rivers. About 900 birds species have been identified in Nigeria.

Below: A secretary bird is on the look-out for a tasty snake. It will grab a snake with its strong claws, hurl it into the air to stun it, and then beat the snake to death on the ground.

Right: A prehistoric-looking pangolin trots across the hot desert sand. It will quickly roll up into an armor-plated ball if threatened by a predator.

Below: A secretary bird is on the look-out for a tasty snake. It will grab a snake with its strong claws, hurl it into the air to stun it, and then beat the snake to death on the ground.

Right: A prehistoric-looking pangolin trots across the hot desert sand. It will quickly roll up into an armor-plated ball if threatened by a predator.

The West African crowned crane *(Balearica pavonina)* and the African gray parrot *(Psittacus erithacus erithacus)* live here. The latter is sadly often poached to be sold into the pet market because of its amazing powers of mimicry – some have developed vocabularies of over 950 words. In the wild, they live in large flocks in lowland rainforests, clearings, and savannahs. They mate for life and can survive for up to 65 years.

The secretary bird *(Sagittarius serpentarius)* has a crest of long feathers that make it look like a Victorian clerk with quill pens stuck in his wig. They eat snakes, snapping them up and gulping them down in a flash, as well as insects, lizards, tortoises, and rats. They stamp on larger prey to kill it first and also drum the ground to flush out prey. They build huge nests up to 8ft (2.4m) across even though they only hold two or three eggs at a time. They are almost completely silent birds, making rare croaks only when displaying.

The forest elephants *(Loxodonta cyclotis)* that live in many parts of West and Central Africa, including Nigeria, are smaller than their eastern bush elephant relatives and have hairier trunks and tusks that point downward, making movement through the thick jungle a little easier. The pygmy elephant *(Loxodonta cyclotis pumilio)* is a subspecies of the forest elephant and is found from Sierra Leone to the Democratic Republic of Congo.

Other animals

The scaly-tailed African flying squirrels are not true squirrels, but are members of a separate rodent family. Nor do they truly fly. Instead, they glide on outstretched membranes connected to their elbows. Found only in tropical Africa, they have rows of scales on the underside of their tufted tails that can cling to tree surfaces

Above: Masks are a traditional part of African culture, used by many tribes during ceremonies, rituals, and dance. This rather lugubrious mask with elongated features is from Senegal.

Left: Boats arrive with fresh fish for the busy market on the Petite Côte at Mbour. Senegal was once the administrative center of French West Africa.

Opposite: A male patas monkey can run at about 35mph (56km/h). Their speed allows these primates to spend more time on the ground than any other monkey.

Above: Lesser bushbabies can leap up to 15ft (4.5m) from branch to branch in one bound. When they venture onto the ground, they walk either on their hind legs or on all fours.

Opposite: *Adult male mandrills have red noses and blue cheeks. Their diet includes small animals, spiders, snails, worms, ants, grasses, roots, and fruit.*

Above: *Helmeted guineafowl are noisy gregarious birds that forage and nest on the ground. They were first domesticated by the Ancient Egyptians.*

Opposite: Ankobra beach, Ghana, where the Ankobra river meets the Atlantic Ocean.

Above: The mud-built palace of Paga Pio, founded in 1620 in Paga, Ghana. It is painted with traditional zig-zags, checker designs, and diamond patterns. Paga is noted for its sacred pond, which is a sanctuary for seemingly 'domesticated' crocodiles.

Following pages: The palace of the Emir of Dutse is the largest palace in Nigeria. It features an amazing array of decoration in blue, green, and gold.

CENTRAL AFRICA

South of the Sahara Desert and west of the Great Rift Valley, this region is dominated by the Congo River and its tributaries, which together drain a vast area that is dense with equatorial tropical rainforests oozing moisture all around – the fifth largest rainforest area in the world. The Congo is the second longest river in Africa (after the Nile). To the north and east lie the Democratic Republic of Congo and the Republic of the Congo. Five of the national parks here are now World Heritage sites: the Garamba, Kahuzi-Biega, Salonga, and Virunga National Parks, and the Okapi Wildlife Reserve. With many areas remaining remote jungles that are rarely visited by man, there are even tales of a strange creature called Mokele-mbembe that some scientists believe could be a surviving sauropod dinosaur lurking in the vast unexplored equatorial swamps!

In this area of abundant lush tropical rainforest there are many fine trees such as the cedar, oak, silk-cotton and valuable timber species like the rich red mahogany and walnut. Palms and euphorbias flourish, and the plethora of flowers whose blooms scent the air include gladioli, lilies, lobelias, and many exotic orchids. Tropical rainforests, flourishing close to the equator, are rich with trees that grow to gigantic sizes, colorful birds, millions of insects, and many animals. Rainforest trees rise above sturdy buttresses with creepers entwined around their tall trunks. Most have dark green shiny leaves that will quickly shed the pelting rain. Orchids and bromeliads grow directly on their trunks and larger branches, and they are pollinated by a myriad birds and butterflies. High in the canopy there are more flowers and fruit and many exotic creatures attracted by these.

The tropical forests of west and central Africa have fewer species of trees than their South American counterparts but they still present a high diversity of types. However, the rainforests are endangered and are vanishing at an alarming rate.

Ethnic groups

There are many different groups and cultures in Central Africa. Notable kingdoms rose and some achieved a high degree of civilization. During the 14th and 15th centuries the continent's center fairly bustled with pastoral tribes who, needing more land for increasing numbers of livestock, gradually migrated farther afield. As the various kingdoms developed, so did their art and warriors: both became renowned. The Bakuba Kingdom (or Bushongo), near the center of the Congo, still boasts a fine administration and is known for its beautiful art, skilled craftsmanship, and vibrant fabrics.

The population of the Democratic Republic of Congo exceeds 59 million and comprises over 250 African tribal groups – 80 percent related to the Bantu tribes. The 700 ethnic languages include the official languages of Lingala, Swahili, Kikongo, and Tshiluba. The Bantu population in Uganda, which includes the Baganda people, numbers approximately 4.4 million, making it the largest ethnic group in the country.

The people of Central Africa now include pygmies such as the Bambuti, the Batwa, the Bayaka, and the Bagyeli ('Ba' means 'people') scattered over many parts of Central and West Africa – in the Democratic Republic of Congo, Congo, Cameroon, Gabon, Central African Republic, Rwanda, Burundi, and Uganda.

Page 102: Lake Hago, Rwanda: open-billed storks use their sharp mandibles to extract snails from their shells.

Page 103: In rural Rwanda, many women weave baskets and mats – and often smoke pipes too!

Opposite: Storks wade among the waterlilies searching for prey in a lake surrounded by lush Central African forest.

Below: Batwa pygmies live in the forests of Central Africa and survive by hunting small game and gathering fruit and plants to eat.

Baka pygmies

Hunters and gatherers in the rainforests, the nomadic Baka pygmies live in traditional huts constructed from branches and leaves. They are built by the women who also weave mats and baskets and keep bees. Baka pygmies live by gathering fruit, mushrooms, and yams, fishing and hunting game with poison-tipped arrows and spears. They sometimes add termites and caterpillars to their diet. Music, drums, and dancing are a large part of their tradition, as are various rituals, initiation rites, and belief in the spirits of the forest. The Baka people of the Democratic Republic of Congo are a separate people, believed to be the oldest inhabitants of the northwestern part of the Congo Basin.

Bakongo

The Kongo peoples migrated here during the 1200s and by the end of the 1900s numbered about 10 million along the Atlantic coast of Africa – from the Congo to Angola. They were ruled by kings and traded in copper and ivory. Today little remains of the ancient Kongo kingdom, except memories that are handed down. Now the inhabitants cultivate cassava, bananas, maize, sweet potatoes, peanuts (groundnuts), beans, coffee, cacao, bananas, and palm oil. Some still fish and hunt – but many now live and work in towns.

Gabon

At the edge of the Atlantic Ocean on the equator, situated between the Republic of the Congo and Equatorial Guinea, this country boasts the largest area of natural parks in the world. The terrain includes a narrow coastal plain, a hilly interior, and forests and savannah in the east and south, although most of the country is covered by dense tropical forest.

The first inhabitants made stone tools here 350,000 years ago and some 2000 rock engravings are testament to these earliest residents. The pygmy peoples were largely replaced and absorbed by Bantu tribes during Bantu migrations. Gabon was discovered by the Portuguese in 1470 and later attracted French traders, becoming a French colony in the late 1800s and eventually gaining its independence in 1960. Today it has some 40 ethnic groups with various languages and cultures, including Baka pygmies, Myene, and Fang peoples who are the largest group at 25 percent of the population.

Today the Fang people live in the hot, humid, equatorial rainforests of Gabon (representing some 80 percent of the population here) and are famous for their guardian figures. These are attached to the wooden boxes that hold the bones of their ancestors, and are reputed to contain the power of the dead. The Fang are renowned warriors who probably arrived here from the northeast centuries ago to farm. They overpowered the local inhabitants and, up to the 1600s, practiced cannibalism. Their leaders (generally descended from the family who founded the village) are believed to communicate with the ancestors of the village by wearing masks – an important element of their culture and art.

Located on the edge of the Congo Basin, its fauna and flora comprise the richest tropical forest complex in Africa, rivaling those of South America – with

Previous pages: As the sunset streaks across the waves, a fisherman in Gabon casts his net into the ocean.

Above: A mixture of sulfur yellow and speckled butterflies gather at a Gabon tropical forest salt deposit. Swallowtails also flash through the sunlit clearings.

Right: The Baka are hunter-gatherers in Cameroon and the Central African Republic. Here a group has set up a temporary camp in the jungle before exploring along a forest stream in search of game.

8000 plant species, 600 bird species, and almost 200 different mammal species. Gorillas, elephants, mandrills, chimpanzees, buffalo, and hippos are all found in this area. The Réserve de la Lopé is Gabon's most accessible wildlife reserve, while the seas are full of marlin and barracuda – and whales which visit from July to October. Other interesting creatures include the soft-shelled turtle *(Apalone triunguis)*, the tree pangolin *(Phataginus tricuspis)*, python, red dragonflies, frogs and toads (some of which have red tadpoles), and catfish.

In Africa the praying mantid (or mantis) *(Mantis religiosa)* is believed to bring good luck to those people upon whom they land. This fascinating little creature is named for its upright stance with arms folded as if in prayer – in fact, it is ever ready to catch a passing delicacy using its front legs which are equipped with rows of sharp spikes. One of the few insects that is able to turn its head, it has huge eyes to spot prey such as aphids and caterpillars. It often moves back and forth, swaying in the breeze like the leaves that it resembles. Then suddenly it leans forward as its front legs snap out to grab an insect. It eats this alive, and has even been known to capture and consume hummingbirds. The bright green praying mantis is found in Gabon.

São Tomé and Príncipe

Off the northwestern coast of Gabon, in the Gulf of Guinea, these two islands form the island nation of São Tomé and Príncipe. They are the remains of an extinct volcanic range. São Tomé sits almost exactly on the equator, steaming in a humid climate. Explored by the Portuguese in the late 1400s, the islands soon became important sugar exporters, and a vast slave population worked there. Later they mutated into transit depots for the exportation of slaves. Coffee and cocoa were grown subsequently and by 1908 São Tomé had become the world's

Above: *A rainforest in Central Africa.*

Right: *The dense green canopy of a tropical rainforest in Gabon.*

largest producer of cocoa. Ethnic groups here today include mixed African and Portuguese-African peoples.

São Tomé is 31 miles (50km) long by 20 miles (32km) wide and is mountainous; its peaks reach 6640ft (2024m). Príncipe is about 19 miles (30km) by 4 miles (6km) in size. Both islands offer a veritable tropical paradise with white palm-fringed beaches, crystal clear water, and unexplored jungle. Streams rush down the mountains through the lush forests and farmland to the sea. Beautiful ferns and a hundred different kinds of orchid flourish in the moist lowland forests, where colorful butterflies dance and birdsong ripples through the trees.

The islands' amazing bird life includes, at one end of the spectrum, the glossy black giant sunbird. Sunbirds are the Old World's version of the hummingbird. They have downward-curving bills that can extract nectar from flowers. Their long, woven nests dangle from the ends of branches. At the smaller end of the scale is the dwarf olive ibis *(Bostrychia bocagei)*. There are also weaver birds, São Tomé thrushes, and black and white São Tomé spinetails on both islands, while African gray parrots preen their fine feathers on the island of Príncipe. At dusk, bats swoop down to feast on the succulent forest fruits.

Meanwhile, São Tomé door snails *(Thyrophorella thomensis)* slowly make their way across the forest floor, camouflaged among the leaves by the colors and patterns on their hard, curved shells that incorporate a hinged 'trap-door' at their openings. They close these doors behind them when they retract to hide from predators – an ability which makes them unique among gastropods.

Democratic Republic of the Congo

This is the third largest country in Africa. Formerly called Zaire, it is now renamed for the word congo (meaning hunter, from the Bakongo ethnic group that live in the Congo river basin). There are more thunderstorms here than anywhere else on Earth and an annual rainfall of up to 80in (203cm) in some places. The terrain is a mixture of plateau, grassland and savannah, steep terraces and high mountains – as well as tropical jungle zones around the river Congo basin and all its tributaries. These cover nearly 400,000sq miles (1 million km²). In terms of its rate of flow and watershed, it is second only in the world to the Amazon.

There are hundreds of species of butterflies to be seen here, and at certain times of the year they seem to fill the sky. There are also many different species of bees, grasshoppers, praying mantids, beetles, dragonflies, scorpions, mosquitoes, tsetse flies, ants, termites, spiders, centipedes, and millipedes.

The existence of the rare secretive Congo peacock *(Afropavo congensis)* was discovered only in 1936 in the Sankuru district of central Congo after Dr Chapin of the New York Zoological Society returned from an expedition in search of the okapi. On his travels he had discovered native headdresses made with unusual peacock plumage – red-brown feathers with black stripes. This furtive bird inhabits the deep forests of the Congo river. The males are mostly dark blue with a metallic green and purple tinge to their feathers, and they have much shorter tails than the Asian species. The hen has a bright chestnut breast and glossy, metallic green back.

The Kuba (or Bushoong)

Today the country is home to many different peoples and ethnic groups but once it was the Kuba who founded a powerful state in the south-central part of the Congo, migrating in the 1500s from the distant north to their present site along the Sankuru River. In time, they absorbed the local Twa people into the Kuba Kingdom which was at its height during the mid-1800s.

The wildlife in this region include chimpanzees and bonobo (pygmy chimpanzees), mountain gorillas, okapis, and white rhinos. The Virunga National Park, established in 1925, is home to forest elephants, chimpanzees, giraffe, okapi, buffalo, and countless birds. Sadly, the pressure of a rising population now facing great economic hardship has driven many Congolese to hunt or sell bushmeat in order to survive. This fact combined with habitat destruction has depleted the gorilla and chimpanzee populations significantly.

The Okapi Wildlife Reserve is a World Heritage site located in forests in the northeast of the country, near the borders of Sudan and Uganda. Over 3000 (perhaps as many as 6000) okapis *(Okapia johnstoni)* live here, together with forest elephant and many primates. The okapi has striped markings similar to those of the zebra – in particular, horizontal white stripes on the back legs – but is in fact related to the giraffe. It unravels its very long (12in/30cm), flexible blue tongue to strip leaves and buds from trees, wash its eyelids and clean its ears. It has short, skin-covered horns and big ears that can detect the presence of hungry leopards. Amazingly, okapis are thought to sleep for only five minutes each day and are always alert for predators.

Opposite: The mighty River Congo is Africa's second-longest river (after the Nile), flowing 2900 miles (4667km) from near the Zambian border to the Atlantic Ocean, sweeping around in a great curve that crosses the equator twice. It encompasses great cataracts, gorges, and rapids, and the volume of water it discharges is second only to the Amazon River.

Below: A male silverback lowland gorilla is the world's largest living primate. A silverback is an adult male gorilla, typically more than 12 years of age and named for the distinctive patch of silver hair on his back. Silverback gorillas have large canine teeth that develop with maturity.

Below: There may be only 30,000 okapis left in the wild. This rather odd-looking herbivore resembles a short-necked giraffe with striped 'zebra' legs.

Right: A mountain gorilla in the Volcanoes National Park, Rwanda. Only about 700 mountain gorillas survive today, and they are only found in the Democratic Republic of Congo, Rwanda, and Uganda. They enjoy eating bamboo, nettles, grubs — and safari ants, scooping these up in huge handfuls until the bites prove too painful to bear.

Above: Enya people set fish traps on stakes in the Congo River rapids.

Angola

Angola stretches along 1000 miles (1600km) of the South Atlantic in southwest Africa. A plateau, some 6000ft (1830m) high, rises sharply from the coastal lowlands. Much of the area is desert or savannah, but there are hardwood forests in the northeast. Many Bantu speakers migrated here from AD 1000 onward and became the dominant group. Angola's name derives from the Bantu kingdom of Ndongo, and the term 'n'gola', meaning king.

For the Portuguese, who discovered Angola in the 15th century, the area served as a useful trading link with India and southeast Asia, and then as a source of slaves for their new colony of Brazil. In more recent times, despite rich oil reserves, there has been much suffering and starvation as a result of civil war. About two million refugees here face a particularly bleak future.

Several decades ago, Angola boasted an impressive variety of game, including elephant, oryx, kudu, eland, black rhino, cheetah, spotted hyena, jackal, lion, giraffe, dik-dik, and wildebeest – most of which have now vanished. Currently,

Opposite: A leatherback turtle has laid her eggs on the beach and now covers the nest with sand before returning to the sea. About seven weeks later the eggs will hatch.
Below: *Oil rigs in the harbor at Luanda, Angola's capital and chief seaport. Angola is rich in natural resources and is one of Africa's leading oil producers.*

efforts are being made to rehabilitate Quiçama National Park and other national parks by reintroducing antelope, rhino, and families of elephant. Over 4000 elephants once roamed here but these have been all but obliterated during Angola's recent war-torn history through a combination of poaching, killing for sport, and landmines. The world's largest concentrations of eland, forest buffalo, and roan antelope have been virtually destroyed.

The giant sable *(Hippotragus niger variani)*, which is unique to Angola, is primarily located in the Cangandala National Park and the Luando Strict Nature Reserve. It is unclear how many are left here, but it does seem to have survived the 30 years of civil war and unrest. This rare creature occurs only in Angola and sports horns that can grow to 5ft (1.5m) in length – making tempting trophies for greedy hunters. Owners of game ranches here have offered up to $1million (£575,000) for live animals.

The small, brown, mouse-eared Angolan hairy bat *(Myotis seabrai)* was discovered in 1912 and is widespread in Central Africa from desert areas to rainforests. It feeds on insects, catching them in mid-air and then dropping the less appetizing hard bits (like legs and exoskeleton) as it swoops away.

Endangered turtles

Several types of endangered sea turtles live in the waters off the Angolan coast, including the olive ridley turtle, but the largest to lay its eggs on these beaches is the barrel-shaped leatherback turtle *(Dermochelys coriacea)*. Adult leatherbacks weigh between 700 and 2000lb (315-900kg) and measure 4-8ft (1.2-2.5m) in length. Instead of a hard shell, their bones are buried in brownish-black skin, with flexible bony plates set on ridges to form a carapace. They can survive in cool waters but enjoy Africa's tropical regions, diving deep – up to 3280ft (1000m) – in search of food like crabs and jellyfish. They are able to hold their breath underwater for up to half an hour and these powerful swimmers have even been known to cross the Atlantic.

Burundi

This small landlocked republic in the Great Lakes region lies next to Lake Tanganyika and is almost in eastern Africa. Formerly ruled by tribal monarchies, it was colonized by Germany in the late 1800s but later fell under Belgian administration and became independent in 1962. Over the years it has witnessed many dictatorships and much ethnic violence.

The headstream of the Nile is located here, as is the western extension of the Great Rift Valley. It features a mainly agricultural and pastoral landscape with savannah grassland and trees which include eucalyptus, acacia, and oil palm. The once extensive forests are now concentrated in national parks and nature reserves. Wildlife in Burundi includes elephants, leopards, hippopotamuses, crocodiles, wild boar, antelope, monkeys, and bushbabies. In addition there are also wild dogs, chimpanzees, and cheetahs. Birds include guinea hens, partridges, ducks, geese, quail, and snipe, which are especially plentiful near the northeastern lakes.

The spotted necked otter *(Lutra maculicollis)* found in this region has light tan-colored fur, mottled with brown spots. They hunt and eat fish while in the water – catching them in their mouths. They can close their ears and nostrils when swimming underwater. They have to keep a watchful eye out for crocodile, or, when they do venture out on land, for large pythons and eagles.

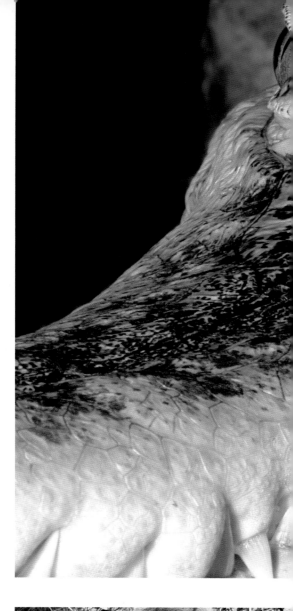

Central African Republic

This landlocked nation of rolling plateau, savannah, scattered hills, high granite plateau, and forest has a tropical climate with hot, dry, dust-whirling winds. In the northwest the Yadé Massif rises to 3750ft (1143m) and in the northeast the Fertit Hills reach 4200ft (1280m) in height and extend into the Sudan. The two largest rivers here are the 807 mile (1300km) Ubangi and the 870 mile (1400km) Sangha, both tributaries of the Congo River. During the rainy season, the Chutes de Boali waterfalls tumble a glorious 164ft (50m).

Over 80 ethnic groups live here, including Baya-Mandjia, Banda, and M'Baka. Sangho is the national language, spoken by most, and only a few of the African peoples here have an elementary grasp of French, the official language.

This country has a healthy population of forest elephants, leopards, lions, and rhinos. Western lowland gorillas *(Gorilla gorilla gorilla)* are found in the tropical rainforests of western Africa, from southern Nigeria to the Congo River, living in groups deep among trees. Only the silverback, or dominant male, is allowed to mate with the adult females when these usually quiet animals can be surprisingly noisy. The offspring are born helpless and must be carried in their mothers' arms until they are strong enough to be able to ride on their mothers' backs – at about three months old – and they will continue to do so until aged about four. Wild gorillas live for about 50 years, eating vegetation, moving and sleeping within a structured family group, led by the dominant silverback. After sunrise, they search for food and eat. At midday the adults usually rest while the younger apes wrestle and play before the afternoon forage. As dusk approaches, each gorilla makes its own nest on the ground or in the trees. These peaceful animals will attack only if provoked, when males will try to intimidate aggressors by standing

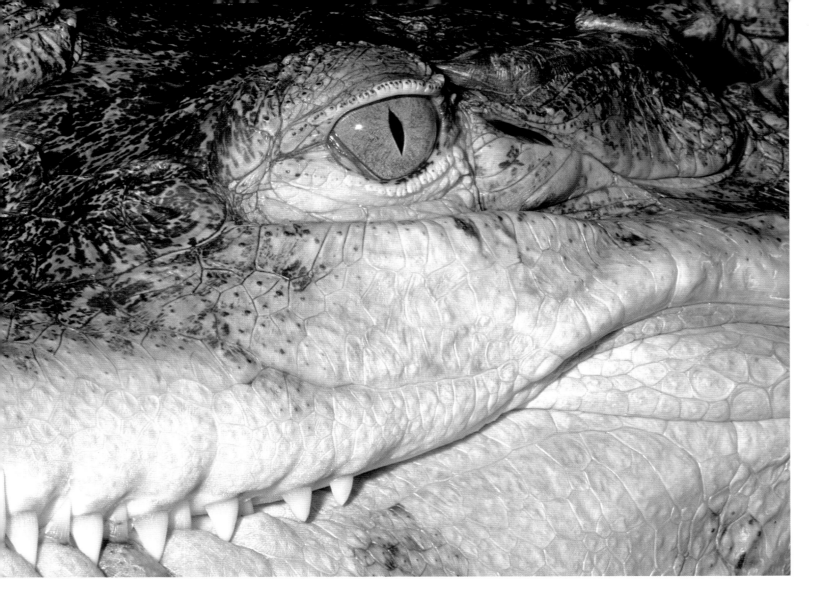

Above: African slender-snouted crocodiles are found in Central and West Africa. These crocodiles live primarily in rivers but have been found in lakes and along the coast. Their diet consists mainly of fish and small aquatic invertebrates; however, the larger crocodiles will eat bigger animals if the opportunity arises.

Opposite: Gorillas can walk for short distances upright on two legs but generally move around by walking on all fours. When doing this, they walk on the knuckles of their front legs. Western lowland gorillas are quiet, non-aggressive animals and there is very rarely any conflict between groups that have overlapping territory. When threatened, the male gorilla will do everything it can to scare off the intruder.

upright, slapping their chests with cupped hands, roaring loudly, screaming, and making charging threats.

Chad

This desert area, 'the dead heart of Africa,' was once inhabited by several quite separate tribes and there are still 200 ethnic groups and over 100 tribal languages spoken in the region. The area around Lake Chad (from which the country's name derives) has been inhabited since 500 BC. Berbers arrived in the AD 700s, and Islam followed in 1085. A strong Arabic influence is still evident as this was once an important crossroads for Muslim traders. It later became a French colony.

The terrain comprises arid plains and desert (edged by the Sahara in the north), dry mountains, and tropical lowlands. Hot dusty winds often blow and drought and locust swarms take their toll on crops and wildlife. Commonly seen animals include antelope, gazelles, leopards, monkeys, ostriches, panthers, and wild sheep. There are crocodiles, rock pythons, and spitting cobras in the Lake Chad region where hundreds of species of birds are either resident or migratory visitors. Terrestrial birds include ostriches, secretary birds, Nubian bustards, and ground hornbills. On the lake there are also marabou stork, shovelers, pink-backed pelican, glossy ibis, and African spoonbills. The lake supports over 40 species of fish, with the lungfish and sailfin unique to this region.

Right: Hippos spend most of the day partially submerged in pools, swamps, and rivers. Here a hippo thrashes through the water in an aggressive display. These are surprisingly agile creatures for their size and weight – and great swimmers. Even on land, they may trot and run when they emerge in the cool of the evening to forage.

Above: The spotted-necked otter is a dark brown mammal with claws and webbed toes. These otters live in many African lakes, especially Lake Victoria. They usually fish early in the morning, striking their prey with amazing speed. They often eat this meal while treading water or floating on their backs.

Left: A group of Western lowland gorillas in the rainforest. Sometimes a male gorilla will launch himself into a pool, making a huge splash to warn other gorillas not to challenge him. His range of calls will alert the group to predators while his chest-drumming display can be heard miles away.

Above: A soldier of the Central African Republic Army. This area has seen great unrest since it gained independence in 1960. A landlocked country, it is home to forest elephants, leopards, lions, and rhinos but years of warfare and poaching have, inevitably, had a serious impact on this wildlife.

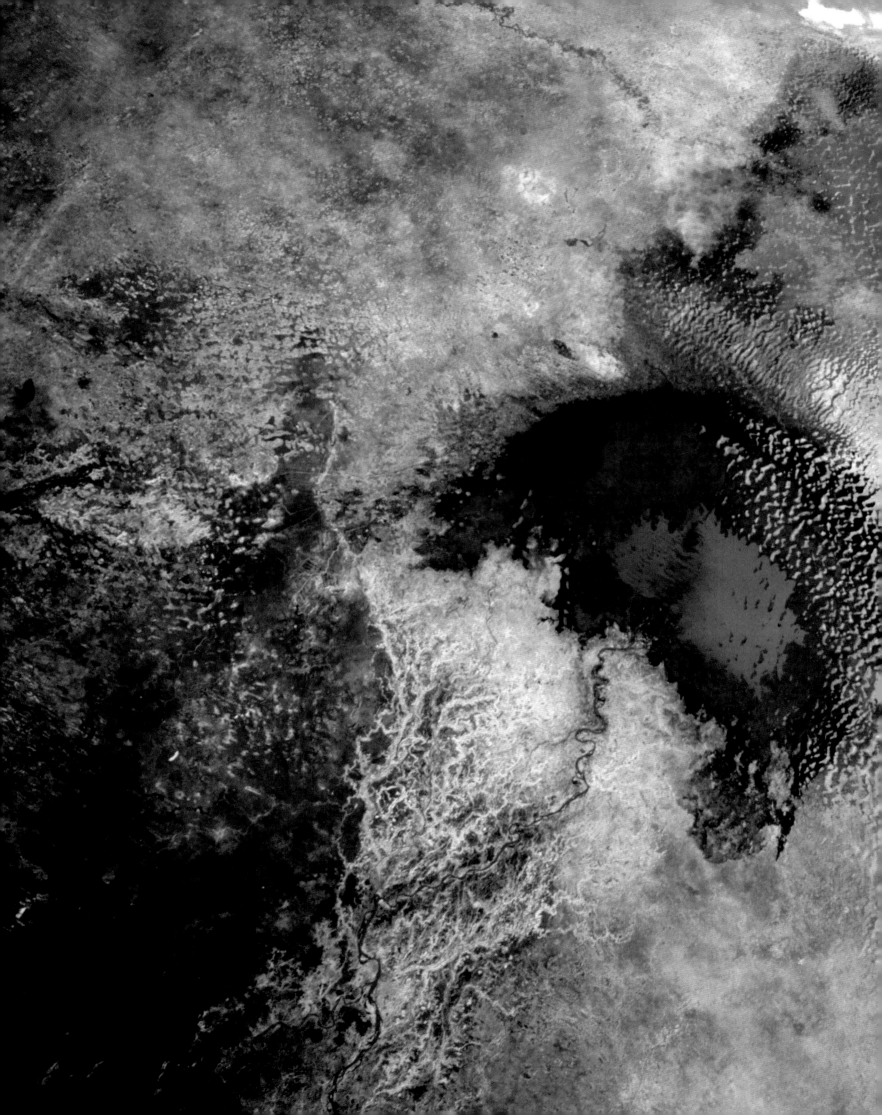

Opposite: *A satellite view of Lake Chad. This is very shallow and is shrinking due to climate change and human use of its water. However, it still supports fish, crocodiles, waterfowl, and shore birds.*

Left: *A saddle-billed stork searches the riverbed for food. It breeds in marshes and other wetlands in tropical lowland, building a large, deep nest (in a tree) in which it lays one or two white eggs.*

This huge saddle-billed stork *(Ephippiorhynchus senegalensis)*, which has a wingspan of almost 9ft (2.7m), breeds in marshes and wetlands in the tropical lowland. It uses its large brightly colored bill to catch fish, frogs, and young birds to eat. This is the largest of the African storks, and is found in Kenya, Uganda, South Africa, the Gambia, Senegal, Côte d'Ivoire, Sudan, and Ethiopia as well as in Chad. Pairs of storks build enormous treetop nests in which they breed.

Common and African spoonbills (*Platalea leucorodia* and *Platalea alba*) have an even stranger bill-shape resembling a long spoon, as their name suggests, that is swept from side to side in shallow water. It is kept slightly open ready to snatch up any small aquatic insects, crustaceans, or tiny fish that may slip inside.

Rwanda

This small landlocked country is set in the Great Lakes region of east-central Africa. It has a fertile terrain as well as swamps, rugged mountains, great lakes and so many hills that it is often called the 'Land of a Thousand Hills.' It encompasses both tropical and temperate regions with snow and frost experienced in the mountains and so many thunderstorms that it is sometimes also described as the lightning capital of the world!

The population includes three ethnic groups: the Tutsi, Hutu, and Twa (an African pygmy subgroup). The Twa were the earliest settlers here, originally living off the land as hunters and gatherers in the once extensive forests. These were cut down eventually, first by the Hutu for farming and grazing, then by the Tutsi for grazing. Today the Twa make up only 1 percent of the total population.

The Hutu, related to the Bantu tribes of Central and East Africa, have lived in the area for some 2000 years as farmers, with both women and men working the land. Hard work is a prized attribute. The Hutu turned large parts of the forests into fields. At 85-90 percent of the population, they form the largest ethnic group in Rwanda.

The taller, thinner, and lighter-skinned Tutsi migrated into the area about 500 years ago. They have a strong warrior tradition and they subjugated the Hutu. They set up small kingdoms and ruled as royalty, establishing cattle ownership as a symbol of prestige which is still in evidence today.

Wildlife under threat

Rwanda is renowned for its unique mountain gorillas in the Virunga Park. Today, the world's sum total of gorillas is possibly less than 100,000 – the numbers of the eastern lowland gorilla having crashed recently. Hunting, logging, and the Ebola virus had already taken their toll and now, as war and mining bring many more people into their range, thousands more may have died. Both the cross-river and mountain gorillas are critically endangered but gorilla-based tourism provides a valuable source of revenue and is carefully monitored.

Sometimes called pygmy chimpanzees, bonobos *(Pan paniscus)* are the most intelligent primates that are found south of the Congo River, and they are also endangered. There may be as few as 30,000 left in the wild. The front-line of the war fought in the Democratic Republic of Congo runs through the heart of their territory. Some are killed deliberately for their meat and others are caught in the crossfire, or mistaken for the enemy and shot. This was the last ape species to be identified (in 1928). It lives in the swampy equatorial forests on the left bank of the Congo River. Bonobos are more slender than chimpanzees with smaller heads and ears, and they can walk upright. They are found only in this small area. Mother bonobos dominate the troop and maintain lifelong bonds with their sons – younger females are sent off to find another troop to join. The troop uses leaves and twigs to build sturdy nests in the forks of trees each evening so that they can sleep in relative safety above the ground.

The leopard *(Panthera pardus)* has a magnificent rosette-patterned coat and long, dark tail. The largest animals grow to nearly 5ft (1.5m) in length, with tails that sweep out an extra 3ft (90cm). Males are some 20-40 percent larger than the females. Leopards usually hunt at night and will take young eland, wildebeest, impala, and gazelle as well as hares, rock hyrax, reptiles, and insects. In these central forested regions their prey includes smaller antelope such as duiker as well as monkeys, rats, squirrels, and porcupines. They drag even very heavy prey high up into the trees to avoid the attentions of hungry scavengers, such as hyenas and opportunistic lions.

Left: *The mountain gorilla has longer and darker hair than other gorilla species, enabling it to live at high altitudes in the Virunga mountains and to travel into areas where temperatures drop below freezing. It has adapted to a life on the ground more than any other non-human primate.*
Right: *A snarling leopard: these cats have strong teeth and jaws that can crunch through thick bones. They are found in most habitats throughout Africa (except for central deserts), wherever there is sufficient cover and prey. They are the only large predators of the rainforests.*

The now critically endangered black rhinoceros *(Diceros bicornis)* once formed large herds that roamed the savannahs until disappearing habitat and poaching for rhino horn reduced their numbers drastically. Now there are fewer than 3000 left in the wild. Its horn (made from keratin – the same protein that makes up human hair and nails) is an important ingredient in Chinese traditional medicine and is also highly prized in Yemen for making dagger handles. After huge conservation efforts, numbers have increased again and black rhinos look set to survive. They eat by browsing with their hooked upper lips (the upper lip projects beyond the lower lip) on small woody plants like acacia, enjoying leaves, buds, shoots, and twigs. They have massive bodies and short stumpy legs and spend a lot of time wallowing in waterholes where the mud sticks to their skin and protects it from the sun's baking heat. Young rhinos suckle their mothers' milk for about a year before they are weaned.

Of the four subspecies, the rarest western black rhino *(Diceros bicornis longipes)* is now restricted to northern Cameroon and Chad and some naturalists fear that it may already be extinct.

The white rhinoceros *(Ceratotherium simum)* is a heavyweight animal more commonly seen in southern and eastern Africa, but some are found in Central Africa, especially in the Democratic Republic of Congo. Its wide squared-off lip allows it to crop a substantial mouthful of the short, green grasses. In fact the name 'white' comes from 'weit,' the Afrikaans word for wide, referring to the shape of its mouth and not its color. Once these relatively gregarious animals were less numerous than the black rhino but this situation has now been reversed. This is the largest land animal after the elephant, with males weighing up to 7716lb (3500kg) and reaching a height at the shoulder of nearly 6ft (2m).

Other Central African animals

The large African bullfrog *(Pyxicephalus adspersus)* can grow to 9in (23cm) in length but may take over 20 years to reach full size. They live in the waterways, rivers and streams of central, eastern, and southern Africa, where they make loud booming croaks. They also spend a lot of time out of the water, using their strong hind legs to dig holes in which to seek shelter and keep cool. These aggressive creatures will fight off predators with fierce determination and can also grip prey tenaciously – they have tooth-like projections in their lower jaw that help them to grasp and chew prey. Their muddy-looking olive brown skin acts as camouflage but, if provoked, they can swell their bodies up to intimidate enemies. During the dry season the African bullfrog hibernates underground, perhaps for as long as 10 months at a time. They are known to stay buried for several years, protected by the mud and lying within a mucous cocoon which becomes hard once dry.

African (or Cape) buffalo *(Syncerus caffer aequinoctialis)* live in large herds of up to 2000 individuals in Central Africa, from just south of the Sahara to just north of South Africa. The forest subspecies, found in Central Africa, reach only about half the size of the savannah subspecies *(Syncerus caffer caffer)*. Mature males of this type stand 5.6ft (1.7m) at the shoulder, with a horn span of 3ft (1m) and they weigh in at up to 1984lb (900kg). All species of buffalo are

Above: *Cape buffalo are powerful beasts with massive upward-curving horns. Males can weigh up to 1984lb (900kg) and are often aggressive, killing more people than either lions or crocodiles.*

Opposite: *Waterbuck live close to water in savannah grasslands, forests, and riverine woodlands. They take refuge in water to escape from predators that remain undaunted by their long horns.*

powerful, aggressive and able to run at speeds of up to 35mph (56km/h). It is claimed that more big game hunters have been killed by African buffalo than by any other African animal, and a wounded buffalo is reputed to stalk and attack its assailant. These huge beasts are quite capable of killing lions, who will wisely single out only the very young, old, or sick individuals as prey.

Male waterbucks *(Kobus ellipsiprymnus)* have splendid, upwardly sweeping horns and all sport long straggly hair that is greased with an oily, water-repellent secretion. They live near lakes and rivers and, while they prefer to stay beside the water or hidden in reed beds, if required they are excellent swimmers which helps them to escape the predatory attentions of lions, leopards, or African hunting dogs. A newborn waterbuck doesn't follow its mother straight away but lies hidden in the long grass for about a month before joining the herd.

Conclusion

Here, in Central Africa, the spirit of Africa has long experienced turbulence and many nations have suffered unrest, war, and political turmoil. Now climate change is set to be yet another threat. Hopefully, if greater stability can be established, more of these magnificent locations will be rescued from the deforestation and species depletion that has become critical in certain cases. Many areas still offer a rich, wonderful, and unspoiled habitat. This region offers the tropical jungles of deepest Africa, fringes of coast, silver rivers, thundering waterfalls, and many extraordinary creatures that live nowhere else. One can only hope that this rich resource of wildlife will survive and thrive.

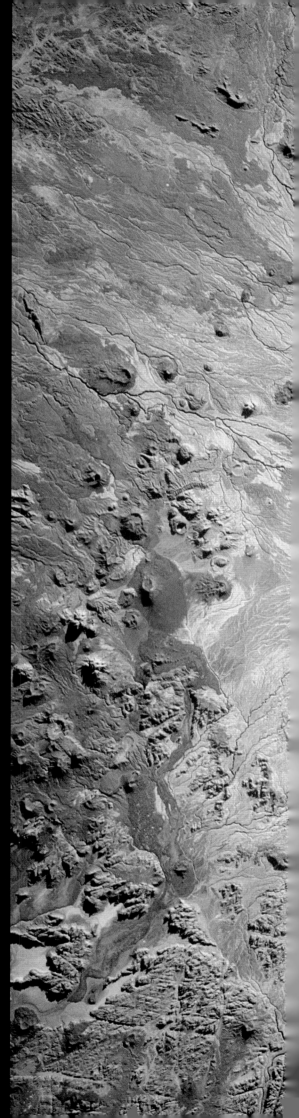

Top: African spoonbill are waders with typically long legs. They live in groups of up to 20 pairs in coastal lagoons, salt pans, creeks, and estuaries.

Above: Aggressive African bullfrogs have loud bellowing croaks. In dry summers they burrow into the soil and wrap themselves up in a watertight mucous cocoon to survive.

Right: A view from space of the Tibesti mountains in northern Chad. It is an area full of chasms and crags, and is home to the Toubou people. The dark area in the middle of this photograph is a dormant volcano.

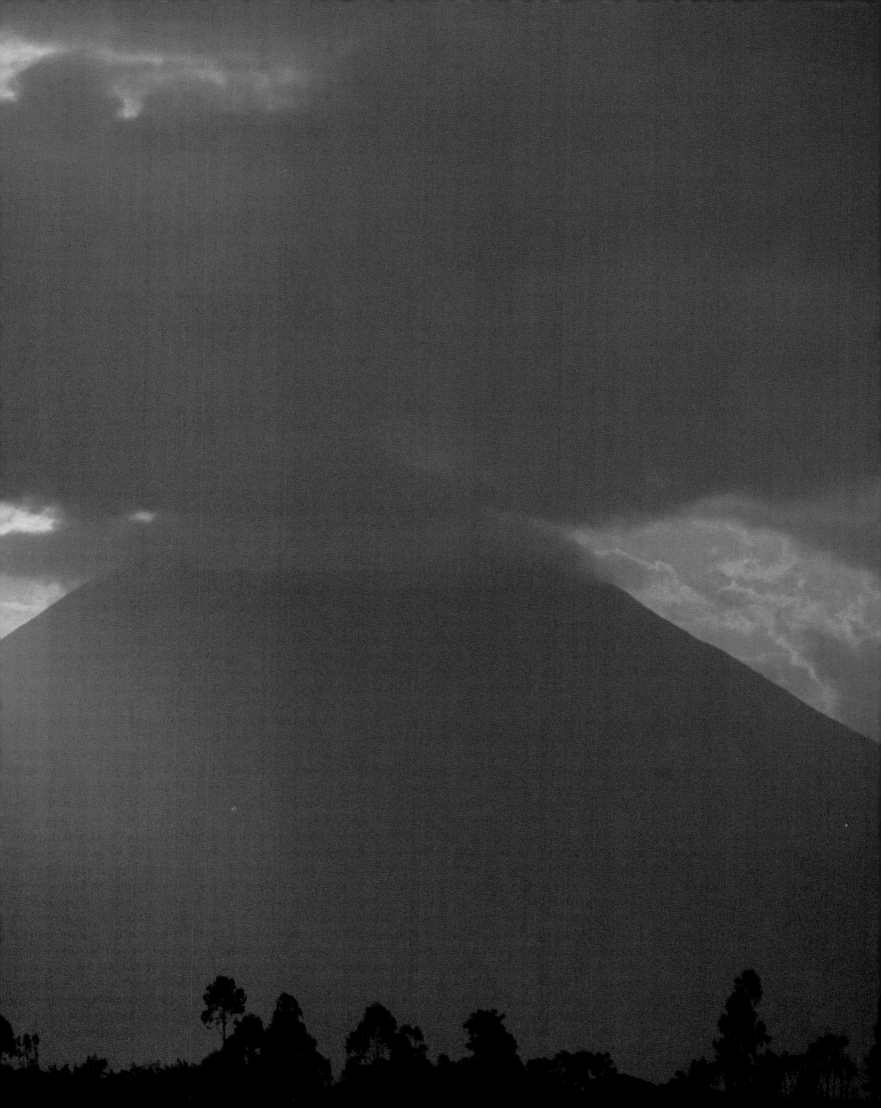

Previous pages: *As the sun sets over Rwanda's spectacular Virunga mountains, the clouds glow like flames. The range consists of eight major volcanoes (most are dormant). Somewhere in the trees lives the endangered mountain gorilla.*

Above: *Topi antelopes in Akagera National Park, Rwanda. Large herds of impala, topi, and zebra graze on the open grasslands in this game reserve. There are also elephants, buffalo, leopards, and hyenas.*

Opposite: *Bonobos or pygmy chimpanzees have smaller heads than the common chimpanzee but higher foreheads. They have black faces, pink lips, wide nostrils, and longish hair.*

Above: Ankole cattle sport impressively large horns. These animals (often called the 'cattle of kings') were depicted by the Ancient Egyptians and their history can be traced back more than 6000 years.

Left: Picking tea in a plantation in Rwanda. Coffee is also cultivated here.

Opposite: An Intore dancer performing the 'Dance of Heroes' in Rwanda. Several centuries ago, Intore dancers (the name means 'The Chosen Ones') used to perform exclusively for the Royal Court in Rwanda.

EAST
AFRICA

East Africa is home to dense concentrations of wild animals, located in stunning scenery that includes vast rippling savannahs, a glorious coast, enchanting islands – and high mountains; Mount Kilimanjaro at 19,331ft (5892m) and Mount Kenya at 17,057ft (5199m) are the two tallest peaks in Africa. Countries in this region include Kenya, Tanzania, and Uganda. East Africa became a prime site for European exploration and colonization in the 19th century.

From the high mountain peaks to savannah plains and tropical coastal zones, a huge variety of plants flourish here, including eucalyptus, acacia, tree lobelia, and oil palms. The baobab tree is an amazing species with a wide twisting trunk that acts like a barrel; it can absorb water from the ground and swell to 30ft (9m) in diameter. The savannah, with its parched grass, low stunted scrub and bush, thorn trees, and skies dotted with scudding clouds is classical safari country – safari meaning 'journey' in Swahili.

A vast number of tribes and different cultures co-exist in East Africa. The Afar people live primarily in Ethiopia, Djibouti, and Somalia inhabiting the Horn of Africa, in forests and rocky desert terrain and salt flats baked hard by the sun and riven by great cracks. They tend their livestock (goats, camels, and a few cattle) and are nomadic, moving from highland to lowlands with the changing seasons and the rise and fall of rivers. Using camels, they transport their simple homes with them, rebuilding these each time they move to a new location. Women milk the goats, make butter or ghee and play music – and generally marry their cousins!

Another important ethnic group in Ethiopia, mainly living in the central highland plateau, are the Amhara. They traditionally wear white clothes and survive in inhospitable mountains where their farms are terraced to prevent

Page 142: Dawn breaks in Tanzania to reveal elephants under an acacia tree.

Page 143: An elephant with her baby in the long grass of the Maasai Mara.

erosion and to retain water. Fields are still plowed using oxen and seeds are sown and harvested by hand – to be threshed by the feet of their animals. The main cooking fuel is farm animals' dried dung. Boys herd cows and sheep, and girls help look after the younger children and carry out chores such as gathering wood, until they reach marriageable age at about 14. They usually are married to husbands just a few years older than themselves.

Bantu

More than 60 million people speak Bantu as their native language. They live south of the Sahara, close to the equator. Over 300 groups (ranging in size from a few hundred to several million) have their own language or dialect and include the Kikuyu, the largest group in Kenya, and the Swahili, whose language is spoken throughout eastern Africa. Many Bantu trace their origins back to ancestors enslaved in the 1700s by agents of the Sultanate of Zanzibar. African slaves were taken from Tanzania and Mozambique to southern Somalia by Arab traders and forced to work on plantations. Today some 120 million Bantu inhabit most parts of Africa south of the Congo River (except for the extreme southwest). There are almost 100 Bantu languages, including Zulu and Swahili.

Kikuyu

Having migrated to Kenya some four centuries ago during the Bantu migration, the Kikuyu (Gikuyu) are a Bantu people, and the largest ethnic group now in the country. Many grow sugarcane, bananas, yams, beans, millet, maize, black beans, and arum lilies which attract bees, white crab spiders and, in the western Cape, a tiny frog known commonly as the arum lily frog *(Hyperolius horstockii)*. The plump rhizome of the arum lily is enjoyed by wild pigs and porcupines and birds relish the ripe fruit. Traditionally the plant is boiled and eaten by Kikuyu farmers. The Kikuyu also raise sheep, goats, and cattle, using cow hides to make bedding and sandals. Some Kikuyu have left their family plots to seek employment in cities or pursue new enterprises, such as politics. The first president of an independent Kenya, Jomo Kenyatta, was a Kikuyu and a vital figure in Kenya's struggle for independence.

Swahili

As Arab and Persian traders established business contacts and married local women on the East African coast, the Swahili community developed – probably in about AD 700, although some scholars think there were Arab settlements here before the advent of Islam. Today Swahili people and culture extend along the coast and islands fringing East Africa, especially in Kenya, Tanzania, and north Mozambique. Some 200,000 to 400,000 Swahili live here now, their name derived from the Arabic word *sawahil,* meaning 'coastal dwellers.' They speak the Swahili language as well as the official languages of their respective countries.

The members of this – the largest ethnic group in northeastern Zambia – scratch a living by growing crops as best they can in the poor soil around villages generally consisting of about 40 wattle-and-daub huts with grass roofs. Each family

Above: The Kikuyu are now Kenya's largest ethnic group, numbering about 3 million.

Opposite: Swahili women wearing traditional black buibui cloaks, paint designs on one another's hands using henna.

grows its own finger millet and cassava and, often also beans, peas, or maize. Once the soil is exhausted, the village is moved – sometimes many miles – to a better location. Malnutrition and tropical diseases, such as malaria and bilharzia, take their toll on the Swahili people and average life expectancy is only about 53 years.

Maasai

The remarkable herders and warriors known as Maasai once dominated the plains of East Africa as their flocks and herds of cattle and goats shared the savannah with the great herds of game with whom the Maasai had long learned to co-exist. A Maasai's wealth is measured in cattle that are guarded from lions in traditional villages built around a central area. These people are renowned for their rich culture, which includes traditional dancing, intricate beadwork, and

Below: Maasai in traditional red clothing. Lion hunting is an ancient custom that played an important role in the Maasai culture. The practice is different from trophy hunting; it is symbolically a rite of passage and ritual that signifies bravery and achievement.

Above: Samburu are semi-nomadic herdspeople who keep cattle, sheep, goats, and camels.

Above: A Maasai mother and her baby.

colorful clothing, in particular their scarlet cloaks. Young males go through a period of warrior training before they marry, at which time they can help to make tribal decisions and care for the cattle. They protect their family herds, and capture other tribe's stock, believing that God gave all the cattle to the Maasai. The women build houses and maintain the home.

For centuries, bands of brothers have been circumcised at the same time (any boy who flinches during this procedure is deemed a coward and a disgrace to his family). This done, the young men become members of the warrior class *(moran)* and must live apart from the village with the other warriors. Eventually they are appointed junior elders and return to live in the village and to marry (band brothers are permitted to sleep with their warrior comrades' wives).

For centuries the Maasai have hunted lions, both as a test of manhood and to protect their cattle. Now it seems that the lions have learnt to recognize their red robes and keep their distance.

Samburu

The Samburu are closely related to the Maasai. They live just above the equator where the foothills of Mount Kenya confront the northern desert, and slightly south of Lake Turkana in the Rift Valley area. Like the Maasai, these semi-nomadic people herd cows, sheep, goats, and camels.

Above: Maasai herding cattle in Kenya. Their lives revolve around cattle whose milk and blood is their staple food. They eat no fruit or grain. Cattle are kept in thorn enclosures at night to protect them from lions.

Left: Maasai wear some 40 varieties of traditional beadwork, usually colored red, blue, and green. Red is the color of the Maasai, blue is godly (like the sky), while green represents fresh grass after rainfall.

Opposite: A Maasai warrior (or moran) scouts the Kenyan landscape. Moran distend their pierced earlobes over a number of years and grow their hair into long braids which are usually decorated with red ocher.

Left: *Samburu boys are taught to herd cattle and goats and learn to hunt in order to defend the flocks. Their sisters fetch water and wood and learn how to cook.*

Above: *A Samburu warrior in Kenya. The Samburu are related to the Maasai and are semi-nomadic herdsmen whose lives revolve around their cattle, sheep, camels, and goats. Samburu warriors have, for centuries, defended their settlements and raided those of their rivals.*

The Samburu eat little meat, making vegetable and root soups, and drinking milk that is sometimes mixed with blood. Most Samburu dress in the traditional bright red clothing and wear beaded necklaces, bracelets, and earrings. Their houses are constructed from plastered mud, or grass mats, or animal hide stretched over a frame of poles. A fence of sharp thorns surrounds the family cattleyard and huts.

The modern world is intruding on this pastoral way of life as new legislation restricts the Maasai lifestyle and they find themselves confined to smaller homesteads. Seeking a role as part of Kenya's tourist industry has, for many, become a more lucrative option, while some of the Samburu people have taken to farming or raising camels.

Turkana

The Turkana are a group of people (estimated at just under one million) who have adapted to survive and live in the harsh environment of northwest Kenya. Their language is similar to Maasai and may have derived from the Nile region. It was not a written language until the late 1960s, when a Catholic priest began studying and transcribing it in order to translate the Bible for the local people.

The Turkana grow crops in small riverside plots and while the men care for the goats, camels, and donkeys, woman make meals, fetch water in containers which they carry on their heads from the river each day, and build houses using branches and palm leaves. Beads and jewelry indicate a woman's wealth and whether she is married or single. The men normally shave their heads or keep their hair very short while women sport a braided mohawk style. The Turkana make marvelous tightly woven baskets – up to 4ft (1.2m) high.

Traditionally, they believe in one creator God and that contact with the spirit world is through ancestors, whom they upset at their peril as sickness or death in the family may result. However, many have now converted to Christianity.

Forest dwellers

Most pygmy peoples live in central and western Africa but some do survive in Burundi and Uganda. They are forest dwellers, with a vast knowledge of the plants and animals in their habitat. They hunt antelopes, pigs, and monkeys for food. They also fish and gather wild yams, berries, and honey, exchanging this forest produce with villagers and farmers in return for crops and other goods. Sadly, those in Rwanda, Burundi, and Uganda have seen most of their forest – and their way of life – destroyed and few now survive. Many have forsaken the shrinking forests to work as laborers – or sadly resort to begging.

Ethiopia

Ethiopia lies just north of the equator, and is the tenth largest country in Africa, with a total border length of 3300 miles (5311km). There are rugged mountains in Ethiopia, some over 13,100ft (4000m) high, as well as sparsely populated lowlands which experience subtropical and tropical climates. In this region are to be found broad savannahs, the Rift Valley with its volcanic lakes, sharp escarpments, sweeping vistas, and an amazing variety of bird life. Fourteen wildlife reserves are home to many animals, including the rare walia ibex and the shy wild ass. After the seasonal rains fall, flowers flourish and reveal the great wealth of native plants.

Left: The Blue Nile Falls (called locally the 'smoke of the Nile') in Ethiopia. It is still an impressive sight in full flow in the wet season, despite the effect of a hydro-electric station, built in 2003, that has now significantly reduced the water levels.

Above: A priest in the rock-hewn church of Abuna Yemata Guh that contains beautiful 15th-century frescoes. Ethiopia adopted Christianity in about AD 333. Some Ethiopians believe that they are descended from King Solomon and the Queen of Sheba.

Somalia

Somalia, situated in the Horn of Africa (an area that resembles a rhinoceros horn projecting into the Indian Ocean) is mostly arid and barren, comprising plateau, plain, and highland. In the far north of the country, the rugged Karkaar Mountains rise steeply. Over the centuries, Somalia's long coastline – nearly 1880 miles (3025km) in length – witnessed trade with the Middle East as well as the rest of East Africa. Once, many lions and elephant, black (or double-horned) rhinoceros, leopards, hyenas, foxes, jackals, badgers, wild dogs, giraffe, and zebra roamed Somalia but their numbers have been reduced during recent conflicts, with some being hunted indiscriminately for food. However, there are still plentiful warthogs, baboons, tree monkeys, jumping shrews, squirrels, and small hares. Some 600 birds and a similar number of plant species are found only here.

Malawi

The south of Malawi supports a dense population and intense cultivation – tea, sugar, tobacco, and coffee are grown. Rural people also plant maize, millet, rice, bananas, citrus fruit, and vegetables. In the north, scattered villages host a traditional way of life, with a strong Islamic influence (especially around the lake) being evident. Christian communities also spread here in the wake of the work of missionaries like David Livingstone. Here roam elephant, lion, impala, and hartebeest, while hippos wallow in the lakes.

Mozambique

This slim country stretches south along 1535 miles (2470km) of Indian Ocean coastline, marking the southeastern edge of the continent. It comprises plains and plateaus, extensive stands of fine trees, rugged highlands, and deep river valleys. The Zambezi River winds its way through to the Indian Ocean along a 62-mile (100km) wide delta. Some of the major rivers in Mozambique are populated by crocodiles. Prawns – transparent as ghosts in the brackish water of mangrove forests where rivers meet the sea – are also found here. There are countless birds, with over 900 species found south of the Zambezi River, while off the coast some 1200 types of fish including mackerel, tuna, and exotic coral reef species thrive in the sea.

Sometimes destructive tropical cyclones strike here, and many temperate forests have been depleted by logging and 'slash-and-burn' agriculture. Woodlands do survive in the southern plains where ancient baobab and mahogany trees flourish. This nation endured savage civil war and strife between 1977 and 1992 that led to gross destruction of Mozambique's wildlife when this was often the only food source for guerrilla fighters. Now native species, including elephants, are being reintroduced into national parks and reserves. Sea mammals, such as whales, dolphins, and rare dugongs, fared better.

Right: Uganda: the sky appears like a glowing orange strip between dark clouds and the River Nile in Murchison Falls National Park.

Left: Livingstonia beach on the shores of Lake Malawi. The lake here boasts an incredible 500 recorded fish species. The town developed from a small mission set up by Scottish missionaries in 1894.

Above: Aloe flourish in Nyika National Park, Malawi, famous for its hundreds of orchids and bird species. Roan antelope, reedbuck, zebra, warthog, and blue monkeys are also plentiful in this region.

Opposite: Cleaning a recent catch of fish at Vilanculos, Mozambique. This coastal town boasts a magnificent beach. The nearby Coastal Wildlife Sanctuary is home to manta rays, reef sharks, dolphins, and a kaleidoscope of fish species.

Above: Margaruque is part of the Bazaruto Archipelago of offshore islands – one of Mozambique's most beautiful scuba-diving destinations where warm tropical waters support many fish, corals, marine mammals, and plants.

Right: Baobab trees with their muscle-like branches are veritable giants, their trunks reaching a vast girth. They provide shade, shelter, water, and food for many creatures – including owls, monkeys, bushbabies, and a variety of snakes.

Above: *This dhow delivers fuel and goods from Vilanculos on the Mozambique mainland to all the islands of Bazaruto. It is beached at low tide to enable loading. Boats like this are the main form of water transport for most local Mozambiquans.*

Left: *An 18th-century Catholic cathedral stands by a palm-fringed beach in Mozambique where Muslim shipbuilders still work. Mozambique was first settled by Muslim merchants and then by the Portuguese from 1505 onward.*

Uganda

British Prime Minister Winston S. Churchill (1874-1965) was so enthusiastic about Uganda's magnificent landscapes, wildlife, and culture that he proclaimed this nation to be the 'pearl of Africa.' Today, the Uganda Wildlife Authority oversees no less than ten national parks, 12 wildlife reserves, and 14 sanctuaries. Uganda is also (with Tanzania) home to Lake Victoria, the largest lake in Africa, with islands that brim with exotic birds.

Situated in the heart of Africa, astride the equator, Uganda is famous for its snowcapped Rwenzori Mountains, romantically dubbed the Mountains of the Moon, where elephant trails still cross the lower forests and chimpanzees frolic near giant fig trees. This country has vast areas of lakes and swamps (almost one third is covered by water), dense forests, woodland, rolling plains, and rich grasslands where elephants and buffaloes graze, and hippopotamus dimple the waters. There are bucks, antelopes, baboons, chimpanzees, colobus monkeys, tree-climbing lions – and the greatest concentration of birds in East Africa, with over 500 species recorded. Uganda is home to half of the dwindling population of mountain gorillas *(Gorilla gorilla beringei)* left in the world (only about 650). A newborn gorilla is covered with black hair and weighs about 5lb (2.3kg). Not until it is about two years old will it be able to reach out and chew on vines and branches. Youngsters do not reach maturity until they are about 10 or 11.

Zambia

This magnificent country encompasses the mighty Zambezi River that rushes to cascade over Africa's biggest waterfall, evocatively called by locals the 'smoke that thunders.' David Livingstone was the first European to witness this magnificent spectacle in 1855 and he named it Victoria Falls after his sovereign. As the water thunders down over the dramatic escarpment, rainbows dance in the mist.

Above: An aerial view from Zambia's side of the spectacular Victoria Falls where the waters roar and crash like thunder as clouds of spray billow up.

Opposite: Victoria Falls: a vast, spectacular curtain of water 5604ft (1708m) wide.

Following pages: Egret and buffalo flourish in Murchison Falls National Park, Uganda. The river attracts antelopes, giraffes, and elephants while denser forest areas provide shelter for chimpanzees.

This nation contains vast stretches of wilderness, grassy plains, thick forests, lush wetlands, and huge lakes, including a small section of Lake Tanganyika in the northeast. This generous mixture of habitats supports many animals including elephants, buffaloes, giraffes, zebra, cheetahs, leopards, hippos, and wild dogs. Here too may be seen the kudu antelope (*Tragelaphus strepsiceros*), with its majestic spiral horns and delicate face, an agile beast that can leap up to more than 8ft (2.5m) into the air.

Kafue National Park is the largest park in Africa, covering 8650sq miles (22,400km²), and is home to many wild animals. Nearly 300 different mammals and 750 bird species – including some found nowhere else in the world – live in Zambia. At night, the red eyes of elusive bushbabies glow high up in the trees and smaller night apes also peep out. They have triangular faces with huge eyes, a long thin tail with a fluffy tip and live mainly in acacia woodlands, where they feed on insects and fruits. The three types of monkey found here are the vervet, the blue, and Maloney's monkey. Zambia also boasts black rhino, huge numbers of crocodiles, and vast flocks of goliath herons.

Kenya

This splendid and very beautiful country straddles the equator, rising from its coastal fringe – where the waves of the Indian Ocean pound the white sand beaches – up to the 17,057ft (5199m) peak of snow-capped Mount Kenya. This is an extinct volcano and Africa's second highest mountain. It is a botanist's paradise as many different flowers grow on its lower slopes. Kenya enjoys a tropical climate: hot and humid at the coast which is fringed with coral reefs and islands but more temperate inland, where the gradually rising coastal plain mutates into a dry region of savannah and thorn bush. It is very dry in the north and northeast. The Kenya Highlands rise up to 2950ft (900m) above sea level.

Kenyan farmers grow tea, coffee, pyrethrum daisies, wheat, and corn. In a hilly terrain strewn with boulders are located the Amboseli Game Reserve (with Mount Kilimanjaro rising above), the Tsavo National Park, and the breathtakingly beautiful Great Rift Valley that slices the Highlands into east and west. The valley runs from north to south through the whole of Kenya.

Early geological upheavals here created a series of lakes – some freshwater, others high saline soda lakes which are rich in algae and tiny crustaceans that are relished by millions of pink lesser flamingos (*Phoeniconaias minor*) that look like rosy clouds drifting across the water. At Lake Nakuru as many as 2 million flamingos gather, joining flocks of pelicans and over 450 other bird species. They share this habitat with lion, leopard, buffalo, and hippo. Rhinos inhabit the safe sanctuaries of national parks in Lake Nakuru, Nairobi, and Tsavo.

In Hell's Gate National Park, where natural geysers spout, eagles and vultures nest high above the grazing giraffe, hartebeest, zebra, gazelle, buffalo, eland, and impala. Hippos (*Hippopotamus amphibius*) wallow in lakes, rivers, and swamps. Despite weighing up to 7000lb (3200kg) these huge beasts can run faster than a human being on land and are excellent swimmers. Perhaps this is not surprising as they are closely related to whales and are even born underwater. They show no

fear of the crocodiles that feed on fish beside them, despite the reptiles' enormous jaws that are ever ready to snap up meatier prey.

Kenya bears witness to the dramatic migration of herds – almost two million blue wildebeest *(Connochaetes taurinus)*, zebras *(Equus burchellii* and *Equus grevyi)*, and other species trek across the grasslands from Tanzania's Serengeti National Park to the Maasai Mara between June and September. When they queue up to cross the Mara river in a huddled jostling mass, hungry crocodiles gather to snatch what prey they can from the heaving throng.

Crocodile embryos do not have sex chromosomes; their sex is determined by the average temperature in the nest during the middle stage of their incubation period. Males are produced within a narrow band of about 89.1° to 94.1°F (31.7° to 34.5°C) and females emerge if the eggs experience either slightly lower or higher temperatures.

Grazing beasts here include waterbuck, reedbuck, Cape buffalo, and the deliciously ugly wildebeest that feeds companionably alongside zebra, both ever alert for carnivores such as lions, leopards, cheetahs, wild dogs, and hyenas. Serval cats and genets also hunt here, plus the much-maligned jackal that, despite its reputation, actually scavenges only one third of its food intake.

Lions *(Leo panthera)* are amazingly common in Kenya. These magnificent creatures (often seen with black-tinged manes in this part of Africa) spend a good deal of the day dozing in the shade (up to 21 hours may be spent lying

Previous pages: *A pod of hippo at Ngorongoro, Tanzania. There are also crocodiles, kingfishers, storks, pelicans, kingfishers, and hornbills here.*

Below: *The hides of blue wildebeest have a silver blue sheen, hence their common name. Young blue wildebeest are tawny brown when they are born, but begin to take on their adult coloration at about nine weeks of age. Adults actually vary in color from a deep slate or bluish gray through to light gray or even grayish-brown.*

around) but are ready to hunt at dusk and dawn. Most prides consist of three males and up to 15 females, plus young cubs, and they can number as many as 30. Cubs born in a pride are twice as likely to survive as cubs born to a lioness on her own. The females make the kills for food, but sometimes the males help by driving the prey toward concealed lionesses.

Lions eat antelope, zebra, and wildebeest (and sometimes even baby elephants, rhinos, or crocodiles) and have been observed occasionally downing buffalo and giraffes. They also catch rodents and reptiles, and steal kills from hyenas and leopards. Lions' eyes contain a horizontal line of nerve cells which enhances their vision when tracking prey across the plain and their roars are loud enough to be heard up to 5miles (8km) away. The Swahili word for lion is 'simba,' which also means king or strong.

Elephants *(Loxodonta africana)* are found from the hot coastlands to the high cold moorlands of the Aberdares and Mount Kenya. These huge, gray wrinkled giants are the largest land mammals in the world – weighing about 12,000lb (5450kg) and standing roughly 10ft (3m) or more tall at the shoulder. They can live up to 70 years during which time they consume vast amounts of food, as they forage for about 330-440lb (150-200kg) of vegetation a day. Females roam in close-knit family herds, dominated by the matriarch, with younger bulls either joining others in 'bachelor herds' or, as older bulls do, living solitary lives away from the others. African elephants flap their huge ears (which distinguish them from their smaller-eared Indian counterparts) to keep from overheating and as a warning sign when agitated. Their dexterous trunks contain over 40,000 muscles.

Top: *Amboseli National Park elephants march across a landscape dominated by Kilimanjaro, Africa's highest peak.*
Above: *The beautiful crowned crane mates for life and lives in grasslands beside marshes.*

Top: When migrating wildebeest have to cross a river, they are vulnerable to attack by waiting crocodiles.

Above: Kudu are elegant antelopes that inhabit rocky hill country or brush-covered plains. The males bear a pair of magnificent spiraling horns.

Left: The glow of a golden sunset makes silhouettes of three blue wildebeest stirring up the dust as they march along.

A giraffe *(Giraffa camelopardalis)* is one of the few animals born with horns. Its scientific name means 'the fast-walking camel-leopard.' These are the tallest animals in the world, an adult male measuring up to 18.7ft (5.7m) from head to toe, and they have the largest eyes of any land mammal. They stride out across the savannah on graceful, slender legs, and can reach speeds of up to 35mph (56km/h). Most of the time they crop the tender topmost leaves of acacia trees using their incredibly long (18in/46cm) black tongues. When they are thirsty, they have to straddle their legs wide in order to bend to drink. They even sleep and give birth standing up. Oxpecker birds often travel on their backs, earning this privileged high ride (and enjoying protection from predators) by pulling out and feasting on ticks from the giraffes' hide. These useful birds make quick scissoring movements through the giraffes' hair, sometimes delving deep into the ears until only their tails remain visible, or nibbling away around the muzzles, eyes, or noses of their hosts.

Great cats

The graceful leopard *(Panthera pardus)* is the smallest and most secretive member of the four 'great cats' (along with lions, tigers, and jaguars) and usually measures up to 6.6ft (2m) in length. Except during the mating season or when rearing young, they lead a solitary life, stalking the dense bush and rocky outcrops in riverine forests. Rich gold in color with dark spots and square rosettes, these powerful cats prowl by night. By day, they sling their long agile limbs over the branches of a tree in thick woodland to sleep in relative security. A leopard is capable of running at just under 40mph (64km/h) for brief periods. It can leap more than 20ft (6m) horizontally and 10ft (3m) vertically and is a fine swimmer. Leopards growl, spit, and make screaming roars when angry or provoked, and like domestic cats, they purr when content. They announce their presence to other leopards with a rasping cough and leave claw scratches on trees to mark their territory.

The cheetah *(Acinonyx jubatus)* is the swiftest animal in the world, and regrettably is now a highly endangered one. With its delicate light frame, it can run in short bursts of about 300yd (275m) at up to 70mph (113km/h). A flexible spine allows the front legs to stretch far forward on each stride and a cheetah can cover around 21ft (6.5m) of ground in one stride. It actually has all four feet off the ground for almost half of this time. Cheetahs have distinctive 'tear-drop' lines running from the eyes to the mouth. These elegant felines survey the surrounding terrain for prey or danger, often resting on an elevated termite mound as a vantage point. A mother cheetah moves her offspring frequently to avoid them being located by predatory lions who frequently kill cheetahs. Cheetahs 'chirrup' when excited or calling to their cubs. They also growl, snarl, hiss, cough, moan, and purr, but they cannot roar like lions.

Left: Lions thrive in many parts of Africa – from the Sahara's southern fringe to northern South Africa. Only adult males boast the full shaggy mane that is characteristic of the species in the public imagination.

Left: *Called the 'greyhound' of the cat family, cheetahs are streamlined for speed. They are lean and fast with very muscular legs. Sometimes mother cheetahs catch live prey so that their cubs can hone their hunting skills by chasing them down.*

Above: *Hell's Gate Park in Kenya offers game and bird watching – or a chance to climb the volcanic remains of Fischer's Tower, regarded by the Maasai as a girl turned to stone. Here hyrax can be seen scuttling among the rocks.*

Tanzania

The coast of Tanzania and the island of Zanzibar were once colonized by Arabs, who had a significant influence on the culture and language here. Centuries later, Tanzania was occupied by the Germans in the 1800s, then became a British territory after the First World War. It finally gained independence in 1961. It is home to over 120 tribal groups (including Maasai) but this is a poor nation and over 50 percent of the population live below the poverty line. The two national languages are Swahili and English.

Set directly south of the equator, Tanzania is renowned both for its great natural beauty and magnificent wildlife. At 19,331ft (5892m), Mount Kilimanjaro is Africa's highest mountain. Its sharp snow-capped peak rises above the savannah – a huge, solitary volcano which is not part of a mountain chain. It encompasses five distinct ecological zones. At the base there are coffee and banana plantations, then forest begins with tree ferns sometimes topping 20ft (6m) and giant lobelia 30ft (9m) in height. At about 9000ft (2750m) the forest gives way to grasslands and shrub where elephant roam. At 13,000ft (3960m) only small mosses and lichens grow, and at the summit are three frozen glaciers and a triple set of volcanic peaks.

Down below, in the hot savannah, the small leaves in the umbrella-shaped crowns of the acacias capture the maximum amount of sunlight.

In 1866-73, David Livingstone traveled through western Tanzania pursuing his missionary work. Here too the paleontologists Louis and Mary Leakey began excavating fossils in the Olduvai Gorge in 1931, their discoveries eventually revolutionizing concepts of human ancestry. Over 130 sites here have yielded bones and tools ranging from 10,000 to nearly two million years old. Some 30 years later, in 1960, another scientist, Jane Goodall, began her famous chimpanzee studies in the Gombe Stream National Park. This research greatly altered our understanding of these apes and also investigated the differences between this species *(Pan troglodytes)* and bonobos *(Pan paniscus)*.

Left: *Tall sandstone pillars at Isimila, a Stone Age site in Tanzania where 60,000-year-old tools were found.*

Right: *Startled Burchell's zebra run through a waterhole. They are named for William Burchell, a keen English botanist, naturalist, and explorer of Africa in the early 1800s.*

Above: Dhows come ashore in the spice island of Zanzibar, which is famous for producing cloves and other spices.

Serengeti

Many safaris to this national park explore the sweeping savannahs which swarm with lion, wildebeest, and gazelle. A Maasai word, serengeti means 'endless plain' and well describes the 5700sq miles (14,760km²) of grasslands that are reputedly home to more game animals than anywhere else in the world. Virtually every African game animal can be seen in the Serengeti – there are over a million wildebeest alone. The Ngorongoro Crater, 12 miles (19km) wide and the largest intact volcanic caldera in the world, is also located here. Scientists think that, before it erupted, it may have stood higher than Mount Kilimanjaro. Today it is ringed with towering walls and forests and its grasslands, fresh springs, and large lake are home to an amazing array of animals – a permanent population of over 30,000 creatures including about 100 lions and 20 black rhinos.

Lake Tanganyika

The first Europeans to encounter Lake Tanganyika, in 1858, were the famous pair of British explorers Richard Francis Burton and John Hanning Speke. Busy seeking the source of the Nile, they arrived at the eastern shores of this vast lake, the world's longest at around 416 miles (670km). At its northern end is Gombe Stream National Park with its forested mountain slopes. These are home to the chimpanzees made famous by the research of Jane Goodall.

Zanzibar

The island of Zanzibar, lush with forests and fringed with palm trees, lies 22 miles (35km) off the Tanzanian coast. Explorers Livingstone and Burton both had homes here. Once this was a slave trade center. Captive slaves would be brought from the interior of the continent, often being transported over 1000 miles (1600km), to be sold – sometimes as many as 600 in a single day. Here too landed ships laden with ivory, and bearing goods from India and spices from the Far East. An Indian bazaar and the world's largest clove market still offer their wares here today where Omani Arabs once ruled and left a fine palace and fort as evidence of their presence.

Other animals of East Africa

This veritable 'Garden of Eden' has an amazing array of animals – and below the hooves and paws of the famous 'Big Five' (lion, leopard, elephant, rhino, and buffalo) is a bustling habitat too, home to countless insects and arachnids, soldier ants, giant millipedes, and scorpions. It has been calculated that in some places, there may be as many as 10,000 termites to just over a square yard of soil surface. Some of these tiny blind creatures (*Macrotermes bellicosus*) raise amazing towers of clay that dot the landscape – gigantic insulated mounds with many partitions and air vents – homes for colonies of workers, soldiers, and their fertile queen.

On the ground, and in the trees, wind a multitude of sinuous snakes, including tree snakes, cobras, mambas (black and green), rock pythons, and puff adders. These are dangerous because once they are settled on a warm patch of earth on the savannah, they are slow to move out of the way, loath to relinquish a

good spot and, if disturbed, likely to strike with amazing speed with their massive fangs, rising high off the ground. They can give birth to up to 150 live young, although about 30 offspring is a more usual number of progeny.

Trees, sky, and many shimmering lakes throng with exotic birds. The superb starling *(Spreo superbus)*, for example, is a stunningly colored creature with glossy royal blue and scarlet feathers. The southern crowned crane *(Balearica pavonina gibberifrons)*, which sports a glorious crest of yellow feathers, lives in grasslands beside the marshes or swamps of Uganda and Kenya. It stamps its feet to disturb the insects it then snaps up to eat. Pairs often display in courtship rituals, their sinuous necks weaving to and fro. The African fish eagle *(Haliaeetus vocifer)* haunts lakes where it not only catches fish but may also scavenge from other birds, and even seize a flamingo as an occasional delicacy. Scavenging marabou storks *(Leptoptilos crumeniferus)* soar high above the plains and they can even catch airborne swallows on the wing. They also come down to the ground to catch smaller rodents and reptiles, and they often haunt garbage tips to scavenge for a rather easier meal.

Lovebirds include the masked variety *(Agapornis personata)* which is found in northeastern Tanzania. These small stocky parrots (up to 6in/15cm long) inhabit dry plateau areas with shrubs or trees for cover, but need to remain near to water as they are always thirsty. If there are farms in the vicinity, flocks of lovebirds congregate to feed on the fields of ripening crops.

Brilliantly colored little bee-eater birds *(Meropidae* species) inhabit lowland rainforests and riverine forests in west and central Africa, Kenya, and Tanzania. Large flocks of several hundred birds hop about in the treetops in between catching flying insects, including, of course, bees and wasps. There are about 24

Above: *Bee-eaters eat a variety of flying insects, particularly honeybees, wasps, and hornets. These exotic-looking birds live in riverbank colonies.*

Right: *Uganda's Rwenzori Mountains rise to 16,732ft (5100m) and include the legendary Mountains of the Moon, famous for their mist-shrouded, snow-capped peaks.*

varieties, all with gorgeous plumage. The hunting bee-eater will snap up an insect in its bill, then return to a safe perch and beat the prey against the branch until it stops moving. A stinging insect is held near the tip of its tail and rubbed on the perch to remove the venom and sting before it is swallowed whole.

Southern ground hornbills *(Bucorvus leadbeateri)* live on the steppes and savannah south of the equator, where the grass is short. This means that its prey of insects, small lizards, and snakes are easy to find. The Maasai believe that these birds should never be killed or bad luck will follow. They even consider that if one lands on the roof of a house, the occupants should move out at once or death will strike. These birds will tackle and consume prey animals as large as hares, tortoises, snakes, and squirrels.

The ostrich *(Struthio camelus)* is the largest living bird in the world, with enormously long legs and neck. A male can reach up to 9ft (2.7m) in height. Ostriches live in flocks of between five and 50, each male mating with his harem of three to five females, but pair bonding with a dominant hen. They lay their eggs in the same nest – a shallow scrape made by the male – but the females can recognize their own eggs in this communal nest.

An ostrich will stretch out its neck and lay its head on the ground to avoid being seen, behavior which gave rise to the myth that they hide their heads in the sand. Thick eyelashes protect their eyes during sandstorms. Ostriches can run at 40mph (65km/h) and their long legs can also deliver a hefty kick against a predator.

Endearing creatures

Several kinds of hyrax are found in this part of Africa – rock *(Procavia capensis)*, yellow-spotted *(Heterohyrax brucei)*, and tree hyrax *(Dendrohyrax dorsalis)*. These rather endearing-looking creatures resemble large, plump guinea pigs and measure about 12in (30cm) at the shoulder. In fact, their closest living relative is the elephant. They scurry about in various habitats that range from high altitudes and cold Afro-alpine moorland to dry savannah, dense rainforest, and even game lodges where they may be seen lounging on the sunbeds!

Jackson's chameleon *(Chamaeleo jacksonii)* is a strange-looking reptile (named for Sir Frederick Jackson, a 19th-century adventurer and explorer) which sports three horns on its head. Like other chameleons, it can change colors and patterning to camouflage itself and has an amazing long, sticky tongue that can shoot out at high speeds to catch its next meal – be it a passing grasshopper, cricket, snail, locust, moth, beetle, or aphid. It has bulging eyes that move independently of one another as it watches for prey and for predators.

Zebras are found only in Africa, living in family groups consisting of a stallion and several mares. Sometimes huge herds comprising hundreds of zebras gather on the savannah where they mingle with wildebeests, ostriches, and antelope – all seeking mutual protection from hungry predators while they graze. A zebra's stripes may serve to confuse the vision of its enemies (lions are their main predators) but they also act as a badge of recognition for the animals themselves. They identify each individual as no two same-species zebras bear exactly the same markings.

Top: Ostriches, the world's largest birds, can gallop as fast as the best racehorses.
Above: A male Jackson's chameleon has three large horns and, like all chameleons, its eyes move independently. It catches prey on a long sticky tongue that it can flick out to full length in a mere one sixteenth of a second.

Conclusion

East Africa positively flaunts a kaleidoscope of different cultures, eco-systems, landscapes, and wildlife – from the snow-capped peaks of Kilimanjaro and Mount Kenya to the Indian Ocean, the third largest body of water in the world. The bush shimmers in the midday sun as lions seek the shade, then cools at night as camp fires flicker under a velvety night sky, and the air vibrates with the chirp of crickets, a zebra barks, a distant lion roars. This really is the Africa of the imagination. It lives up to the dream. It encapsulates the spirit of the continent as a child's book might depict it – a tapestry of wild animals woven into a magical landscape.

Above: A Burchell's zebra trots below towering Mount Kilimanjaro, whose name means 'shining mountain.' It is thought that this is the tallest free-standing mountain in the world, rising to 19,331 ft (5892m) from the equatorial jungle lapping at its base to its snow-capped summit.

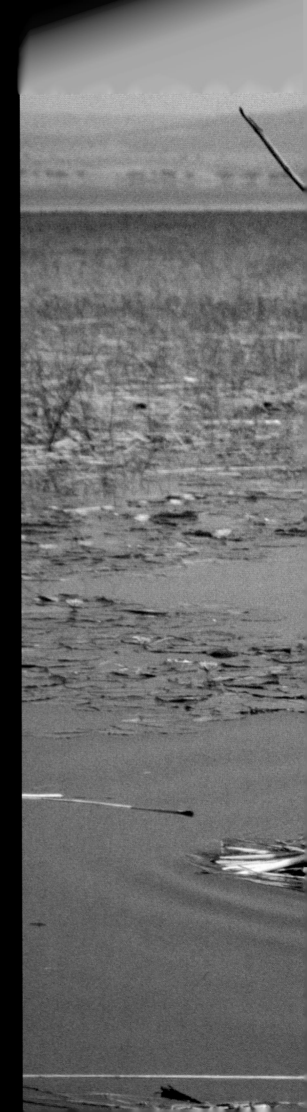

Above: An Afar man sports an impressive dagger. These nomadic pastoralists raise goats, sheep, and cattle in the desert. The Afar Depression in the Horn of Africa includes the lowest point in Africa, Lake Assal. It is one of the hottest places in the world.

Left: Mursi women from the Omo Valley in southwestern Ethiopia have elaborate facial tattoos and huge clay lip plates (inserted into slits in their lower lips). Their territory is bounded by three rivers and a mountain range that isolates them from the rest of the world.

Right: A man maneuvers a small papyrus boat as he collects reeds in Lake Awassa, Ethiopia, the smallest of the Rift Valley lakes.

Previous pages: Wildebeest at sunset in Amboseli National Park in Kenya. Sometimes also called gnu, these odd-looking beasts keep on the move continually in their quest for grass and water.

Previous pages: Lesser flamingos in Lake Magadi, Kenya. This is an alkaline soda lake surrounded by salt flats. The birds live in salty lakes and lagoons, eating algae, small insects, mollusks, and crustaceans.

Above: Unusual-looking Senecio kilimanjari plants grow in the moorland zone of the mountain after which they are named. Giant lobelias grow up to 10ft (3m) tall here, too, and the air is scented with the fragrance of many different plants.

Left: Mount Kenya is an extinct volcano set close to the equator. The park, made a World Heritage Site in 1997 by UNESCO, includes high forest bamboo, alpine moorlands, glaciers, tarns, and glacial moraine.

Right: Mount Kilimanjaro extends for some 50 miles (80km) and comprises three extinct volcanic cones. The highest (and youngest) cone is named Kibo. Shira to the west and Mawenzi to the east are the older cones that make up the giant stratovolcano.

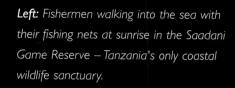

Above: For centuries, the inhabitants of Zanzibar and Pemba cultivated spices, but now the women may be found tending seaweed beds at low tide. The crop is dried, baled, sold, and then shipped around the world for use as food, clothing, and medicine.
Following pages: Acacias backlit by a golden Serengeti sunset.

SOUTHERN AFRICA

This region, at the southern tip of the continent, rich in resources, wildlife, and gold, was long dominated by European rule, in particular the British and Dutch. However, the 20th century ushered in great changes and most nations in Southern Africa had achieved independence by the 1960s. Zimbabwe gained majority rule in 1980, and Namibia finally freed itself of South African domination in 1990.

This southern region has a magnificent landscape – its dramatic coastline, mountains, and high veldt all offering inspiring vistas and an unrivaled variety of splendid habitats for wildlife. South Africa itself is bordered by the Atlantic Ocean to the west and the Indian Ocean to the south and east. Along its northern border lie Namibia, Botswana, and Zimbabwe, with Mozambique and Swaziland to the northeast and the independent kingdom of Lesotho enclosed in the eastern central plain. The Zambezi river originates in northwestern Zambia, formerly Northern Rhodesia, and flows through Angola, Botswana, and Zimbabwe to Mozambique. Offshore to the east is Madagascar which is home to many amazing creatures, many of them unique as a result of the island's geographical isolation. Three-quarters of its estimated 200,000 plants and animals are not found anywhere else in the world.

Flora

Some ten percent of the world's flowering species of plants are found in South Africa, and the Cape Peninsula alone boasts more plant species than the whole of Great Britain. The flowers here are as glorious and colorful as the lands and people of the region, typified by the red poinsettia and the bright golds, reds, purples, and icy whites of osteospermum and gazania. Here too grow flamboyant, succulent mesembryanthemums with their glistening leaves and petals, and their relatives, the stone plants, dwarf succulents that thrive in arid or desert environments. Sweetly fragrant freesias originate from Southern Africa, as do many delicate ericas (the largest genus of flowering plants in South Africa), agapanthus, gladioli, pelargoniums, and arum lilies.

Silver trees *(Leucadendron argenteum)* grow in the Cape peninsula, as do coast silver oaks *(Brachylaena discolor)* with their striking silvery blue foliage, while the exuberant bird-of-paradise bloom *(Strelitzia reginae)* mimics the shape of its avian namesake's head and neck, and bears orange and blue flowers. *Strelitzia nicolai* is a giant version with blue and white flowers. These are just two examples of the many crane flowers to be found here, many pollinated by sunbirds which use their long, curved beaks to probe the bracts for the delicious nectar.

The king protea *(Protea cynaroides)* is the national flower of South Africa and it can grow up to 6.6ft (2m) high, with vast flower heads about 12in (30cm) across. This plant is widely distributed in the southwestern and southern Cape where the Cape Floral Region is classified as a Unesco World Heritage site. The proteas gave their name to South Africa's national cricket team.

In Namaqualand, a dry, rocky semi-desert stretches for 600 miles (965km) along the western edge of South Africa. This barren place flowers prodigiously for just a few short weeks in the spring when it is transformed into dazzling sheets of color. Golden yellow and orange Namaqualand daisies predominate, but there are also iridescent succulent mesembryanthemums and the lovely quiver tree *(Aloe dichotoma)* – a huge aloe. Its fibrous stem was used by native bushmen to make quivers to hold their arrows. Here too grows a bizarre tall succulent with a human-like shape, colloquially called the halfmens *(Pachypodium namaquanum)*.

Welwitschia mirabilis is a huge plant found in the Namib Desert. It is renowned for its longevity – in fact it is one of the longest-lived in the plant kingdom. Some are a mere five or six centuries old, but their lifespan can exceed 1500 years. Their long, strap-like leaves creep along the ground, splitting into segments as they are whipped and twisted by fierce winds. The plant can produce over 492ft (150m) of leaf tissue over a growth period of 1000 years.

The real yellowwood *(Podocarpus latifolius)*, South Africa's national tree, can grow up to 130ft (40m) tall, but more often the trees are found clinging onto exposed mountain slopes and so are short, bushy, and gnarled, with deeply split bark that peels off in strips.

Ethnic backdrop

Many peoples with diverse cultures live in Southern Africa. Today, the largest of the many different ethnic and language groups are Zulu, Xhosa, Tswana, and Bapedi, but people have been living in Southern Africa for 100,000 years or so.

It is the San people in the Kalahari Desert who are the oldest known settlers here. They are bushmen who have been inhabitants of Southern Africa for over 20,000 years. Aboriginal hunter-gatherers, famous for their click consonant language, their domain once stretched from the Zambezi to the Cape of Good Hope. Now Southern Africa's bushmen face extinction. The last 600 or so Gana and Gwi and the remaining San of Botswana's Central Kalahari Game Reserve are

trying to regain the right to roam freely in their lands, despite Botswana's central government trying to move them out of the Central Kalahari Game Reserve in the mid-1990s. This reserve was originally created 30 years earlier to protect the 5000 bushmen living there.

Bantu

Some 2000 years ago, Bantu-speaking tribes from Central and West Africa arrived bearing their knowledge of cattle farming and iron-smelting. Today the term Bantu refers to both the tribes and the language.

From the early Bantu people, the Nguni descended – and then, eventually, the Zulu. These people measured their wealth in cattle, a tradition that continues today. The Nguni traveled east and southeast from the Great Lakes some 2000 years ago. The women carried their belongings on their heads, while young boys drove the animal herds ever onward. Ultimately they reached the lush tropical coastal strip beside the Indian Ocean and many prospered here under a king who gave the region its name, Maputaland. Some brave individuals explored yet farther, discovering good fertile land irrigated with rivers and streams – and no tsetse fly to infect their livestock.

The Karanga, meanwhile, had headed south into today's Zambia and Zimbabwe, some eventually confronting the 'ancient' San or Bushmen there. The Karanga people ruled a great inland African empire from about AD 1000 to AD 1600. They smelted gold and traded it on the shores of the Indian Ocean. Vast stone ruins have survived. They were called Great Zimbabwe, the term Zimbabwe meaning 'stone dwelling' in the native Bantu language. The present name of the nation has descended from this fine heritage.

Page 198: A zebra's stripes are an effective form of camouflage, particularly in tall grass.
Page 199: A dawn mist fills hollows in the Namib Desert – home to the world's highest sand dunes.

Left: Namaqualand bursts into spring color with a living carpet of wildflowers.
Above: The Namib Desert: contorted strands of Welwitschia mirabilis *that can live for anything up to 1500 years.*

Left: *Animal spoor is checked out by Kalahari bushmen. The San are the most ancient residents of Southern Africa – they have lived here for at least 20,000 years. Formidable trackers and hunters, they can follow animals across most terrain and are able to distinguish between the spoor of a wounded animal and the rest of the herd.*

Above: *Bushmen sitting outside their grass homestead in the Kalahari. San villages range in sturdiness from simple nightly rainshelters in the warm spring, when the people move constantly in search of budding green plants, to formalized rings of huts when they congregate in the dry season around the only permanent waterholes.*

Xhosa

The Xhosa, or 'Red Blanket People' (ocher red and orange are their traditional colors), have Bantu origins and sprang from the Nguni clans. Later, a second group of Nguni-speakers joined them, but were driven out of Zululand by Shaka, the Zulu king. Some would return when peace was declared while others were assimilated into the Xhosa nation – the second largest group of black Africans in South Africa, and the only ones never defeated or enslaved by another tribe. They even kept the mighty Zulu chief, Shaka, at bay. Today, the Xhosa live mainly in the Eastern Cape Province, where once they sought refuge in forests when frontier wars raged. But often the strife followed them into the trees which are now said to be full of spirits from these mighty battles. Today they live in the southern and central southern parts of the country, farming, grazing their cattle, and growing tobacco.

The ancestors of the Sotho people migrated south of the Limpopo River and eventually dispersed over the vast interior plateau. Those who settled in the western regions were called Batswana (Tswana) and those in the southern regions, Basotho. Botswana means 'Land of the Tswana'.

Tswana

Tswana states developed through royal control of cattle as well as by exploiting their expertise in mining, manufacture, and trade. The Tswana were settling on the Highveld from at least the 1600s. For 200 years or so chiefdoms split, creating ever smaller chiefdoms and overlapping 'city-states.' Successive disputes and wars further weakened them until, in 1810, the warriors of the Zulu King Shaka annihilated scores of tribes. Wide areas of grassland were cleared of cities and people, until only stone ruins remained. Those Tswana that survived eventually returned to cultivate their lost lands some 30 years later, and then they allowed Boer migrants to settle on the Highveld too. Today, the Tswana live in parts of Gauteng Province (around Johannesburg), the Northwest Province, and eastern Botswana. Today Botswana is inhabited by people of predominantly Tswana origin.

Sotho

Several waves of the Sotho people migrated south from the Great Lakes in Central Africa about 500 years ago. The last group (the Hurutse) settled in the Western Transvaal toward the beginning of the 1500s. The Bapedi descended from them but many were killed or displaced by the Zulus.

The Sotho or Basotho (modern Lesotho) people arrived in southern Africa in the 1400s. Most Sotho herded cattle, goats, and sheep, and grew grains and tobacco. Skilled craftsmen, they were renowned for their metalworking, leatherworking, and carving of wood and ivory. Various clans were gathered together in the early 1800s by their great chief Moshoeshoe I, who established their nation and invited in missionaries, probably hoping thereby to gain access to European guns. In 1843, the Basotho allied with the British Cape Colony. Today at least seven million people who speak Sotho or related languages live in South Africa. Some three million more live in neighboring countries.

Opposite: The painted face of a young Xhosa in the Eastern Cape region of South Africa. He is celebrating his recent circumcision that marks his initiation into manhood.

Above: A Basotho man in Qwaqwa, which was a homeland created for the southern Sotho people from a reserve in the Orange Free State. It was reunited with South Africa in 1994. The Basotho Cultural Village explores their lifestyle and architecture from the 1500s to today.

Following pages: Zulu dancing — associated with hunting, courage, and war — is exciting, energetic, and rhythmic as the warriors, dressed in traditional costume, brandish their spears and shields.

Opposite: The setting sun paints the waters of Lake Kariba a dusty pink.

Below: 'Throwing the bones' in Swaziland: the various patterns that they make are used as a means of divination.

Ndebele

The Ndebele people of Zimbabwe are also known as the Matabele, a branch of the Zulus who in the 1820s had separated from King Shaka to follow a rival leader, Mzilikazi. They moved to the Pretoria area, met the Tswana people, and then moved north into today's Zimbabwe, where they fought the Shona but eventually settled in what is now Matabeleland.

Swazi

The Swazis are a Bantu-speaking people and are part of the Nguni ethnolinguistic group. They originated from east central Africa, crossing the Limpopo River and settling in today's Mozambique in the late 1400s, and then moved into the Pongola River region before battles with the Ndwandwe people drove them into the central area of modern Swaziland. Here they conquered many small Sotho- and Nguni-speaking tribes and today's Swaziland emerged.

Tsonga

In the early 1500s, the Portuguese reported that Tsonga inhabited the central and southern areas of Mozambique. An isolated peaceful people, they lived in scattered settlements, until the Nguni, displaced by Shaka, the Zulu king,

subjugated them. They eventually reigned over a region stretching from the Zambesi River to Delagoa Bay (today's Maputo). After clashes in the 1830s, some groups settled near the present-day Kruger National Park. Throughout the 1800s, Tsongas hunted elephants and sold the ivory to traders. As elephant herds diminished, they hunted smaller game like buck instead and traded skins, furs, and horns, They enjoyed venison and, using conical plunge baskets, caught fish trapped in shrinking lakes during the height of summer. Today, small numbers inhabit the Northern Province – living in central and northeastern regions, as well as parts of Swaziland, Zimbabwe and Mozambique. Many practice Christianity, as well as traditional ancestor worship.

Venda

The Venda people live in the northern Transvaal and have their own language. Originally hunters and farmers, they kept cattle and goats and made their homes in large mountainside villages ruled by a chief and council. These remote locations made them the last of the Bantu-speaking peoples of South Africa to encounter Europeans and so they were less affected by the influence of these new cultures.

Zulu

The Zulu people are the largest ethnic group in South Africa, renowned for their history of warfare and their conquest of a large domain. For Zulus – and Matabele – the art of war and military strategy was a science and a way of life. During the early-1800s, these powerful people developed war skills under their king, Shaka, who transformed a small obscure tribe into a mighty regional power. In due course, they conquered vast territories, including Mozambique and Zimbabwe; they overcame the Batswana, Shona, Basothos, Batau, and Bapedi people. Few enemies escaped their spears and swords.

Under the great chief Cetshwayo, in the Zulu War of 1879, Zulu warriors came into conflict with the invading British troops. History tells of massive slaughter of British soldiers at the battle of Isandhlwana – as well as the famous British stand at Rorke's Drift garrison, when just 139 (mainly Welsh) soldiers, of whom 35 were patients in the hospital, held out against an attack by more than 4000 Zulu warriors, losing only 17 men during the six waves of the battle – a feat resulting in the award of 11 Victoria Cross medals for the soldiers and even honored by the Zulus themselves.

The Zulu were stirred into battle readiness by the beat of drums. Drums were also used as a means of healing, with drum beats believed to soothe both mind and soul. Dancing is central to Zulu culture and their traditional dances include the hunting dance, when they use sticks to mimic spears, and the rhythmic 'dance of the small shield' used since the time of Shaka Zulu to encourage military unity. Today, it is normally performed at royal occasions. Zulu culture prizes the making of beautiful brightly colored beads, baskets, and small carvings. It is estimated that about 7.5 million Zulu live in KwaZulu-Natal, as well as some in Zimbabwe, Zambia, and Mozambique. Their language is the most widely spoken in South Africa.

Left: *Cairns of white stones and memorials mark the site of the Battle of Isandhlwana in the 1879 Zulu War. Some 20,000 Zulu warriors killed most of the 1700 British soldiers ranged against them. The Zulu rear guard then attacked the nearby mission station at Rorke's Drift where a tiny force of British soldiers successfully defended their garrison against four to five thousand Zulu warriors.*

Above: *A Zulu wearing traditional costume. The Zulu warrior at the time of Rorke's Drift was not a professional soldier but was a formidable foe nonetheless. The Zulus were a citizen army called up in times of war, although all Zulu men were required to do military service when they reached the age of 19 until the age of 40, when they were allowed to marry and passed onto the Zulu reserve list.*

Zimbabwe

Formerly known as Southern Rhodesia, this nation is bounded by rivers, its northwest border being edged by the Zambezi river and its southern frontier by the Limpopo. The incredible Bridal Veil Falls are a famous landmark in a rich habitat that supports elephants, sable antelope, vervet monkeys, lions, buffalo, hippos, rhinoceros, gorillas, chimpanzees, giraffe, waterbuck, zebra, warthogs, and otters. Scaly anteaters are also found here: they have sharp overlapping armored scales that make them look rather like artichokes strutting about on legs. Like skunks, these pangolins can spray a noxious liquid when attacked, so they are well protected from predators on several fronts!

Baboons are the largest members of the monkey family, with long dog-like muzzles and heavy 'frowning' brows. Some species sport bright patches of red, blue, or purple skin on face, chest, and rump. They live in well-organized troops under the scrutiny of dominant males who keep order between quarrelsome members, protect the group from predators, such as leopards, and lead them into the safety of trees or cliffs at night. Baboons have strong fangs which they bare at enemies, or use to challenge a member of the troop. They walk on all four limbs with their tails held up in a confident arch.

Botswana

This landlocked nation has gently rolling tableland and is dominated by the Kalahari Desert that covers 70 percent of it. This huge sand basin stretches from the Orange River up to Angola, and is dotted with sand dunes, ancient dry riverbeds, gravel plains, dry grassland, and scrubby acacias. It is really semi-desert as it does receive over 10in (25cm) of rain each year. Animals seen here include brown hyenas, lions, oryx, and meerkats.

The world's largest inland delta, Okavango, lies to the north of Botswana, as does the vast saltpan called Makgadikgadi. Blue wildebeest and antelope roam the savannahs and there are more elephants in Botswana than anywhere else in the world – about 120,000 of them.

Above: *Lions are one of the 'Big Five' animals that every tourist hopes to capture on camera, and which are found in abundance in Zimbabwe and Botswana.*

Right: *A family group of elephants take a drink at a waterhole in Botswana. There are more elephants in Botswana than anywhere else on Earth.*

Opposite: *The floodplains of the Okavango Delta in Botswana, the world's largest inland delta. Here the freshwater floods inland, creating a tangle of lagoons and channels in the Kalahari sand.*

Left: *Victoria Falls amazed David Livingstone when he first saw the 'smoke that thunders' in 1855, having heard their tumultuous roar while still miles away. He caught his first glimpse of the falls from Livingstone Island, in the middle of the Zambezi River.*

Above: *Zimbabwe's Bridal Veil Falls tumble 164ft (50m). This is an area of rugged grandeur with deep gorges and many splendid waterfalls. Villages in Zimbabwe typically contain round huts with earthen walls and thatched roofs.*

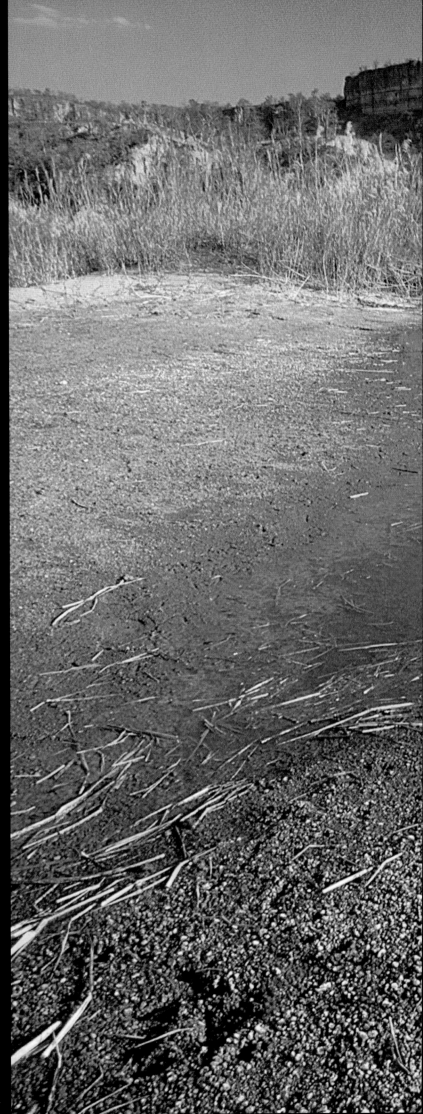

Right: Zimbabwe: lions' spoor dot the ground near the water's edge by the magnificent red sandstone Chilojo Cliffs. They are visible 30 miles (50km) away and are especially beautiful in the rosy light of sunset or dawn.

Above: The handsome sable antelope of Southern Africa belongs to a group called sabre-horned antelopes, because of their long, scimitar-shaped horns. Those of the sable antelope are covered with distinctive ring-like ridges.

There are 164 different kinds of mammals in Botswana. One of the most engaging is the meerkat *(Suricata suricatta)*. They habitually dig burrows and tunnels for their colonies in grassland areas, and then post guards to defend these. There is always at least one male watching out for danger. Meerkats are a type of mongoose, some 10in (25cm) long with tails almost as long again. They have pale sandy fur, brown stripes, and sharp snouts. Their dextrous front feet can pick up objects, and they also use them to groom their neighbors.

Leaving male and female baby sitters to keep an eye on the young pups, meerkats emerge from their burrows at sunrise once they are sure the coast is clear, and then spend most of the day foraging for spiders, grubs, moths, crickets, caterpillars, mice, lizards, small birds, roots, and melons to eat – they even enjoy the occasional snake and scorpion. Those posted on sentry duty climb to a high vantage point to scan the terrain, standing upright on hind legs, and making loud warning cries should a predator be spotted.

The Latin name for African hunting dogs *(Lycaon pictus)* means 'painted wolf-like animal' – an apt description of their mottled black, brown, and beige coats. They have large, rounded ears, dark brown circles around their eyes, and only four toes instead of the usual 'dog-family' five. Between 2000 and 5000 remain in the wild, but they are only found south of the Sahara on savannahs, grasslands and open woodlands where the packs hunt antelope, zebras, wildebeest, springboks, gazelles, and impala. Normally only the alpha male and female breed while other members of the pack help to care for the litter. As many as 16 pups may be born, but usually only a few survive to maturity.

The bat-eared fox *(Otocyon megalotis)* has large ears – up to 5in (13cm) long, a short narrow mouth set in a raccoon-like 'face-mask' and long jackal-like legs. It feeds mainly on insects, with a particular liking for grasshoppers, dung beetles,

Above: Meerkats on parade: this co-operative mongoose is often seen on guard duty while others in the group hunt for juicy beetles, worms, lizards, larvae, and even scorpions to eat. The guards watch out for an eagle or a jackal, sound a warning bark if they spot one, when the troop dashes for cover into a nearby burrow.

Left: Bat-eared fox cubs are often cared for by their fathers while the females hunt for food, such as termites and beetles, plus a few mice and lizards. They will leap high to catch grasshoppers and winged insects.
Opposite: Wild dogs live in small packs comprising a dominant breeding pair, pups, and a number of non-breeding adults. They roam over plains and bush, hunting in the morning and early evening. Once the prey is killed, youngsters are allowed to eat first.

and termites, but it will also eat small mammals, lizards, birds, eggs, or any fruit that it comes across. It is able to chew by opening and closing its jaws up to five times a second. These nocturnal foxes live in pairs, and both partners help to rear the cubs.

The spotted hyena *(Crocuta crocuta)* is Africa's most common large carnivore, and was once domesticated in ancient Egypt – in those times it was often reared and fattened for human consumption. In a rare turnabout, female spotted hyenas are larger than and dominant over the males and even their external genitalia bear a marked similarity to those of the male. These scavengers are capable of bringing down prey as large as a zebra and have incredibly powerful jaws in relation to their size.

By day hyenas sleep in rocky dens or holes in the ground, and emerge at night to hunt in packs, chasing their victim until it is exhausted – when they down and disembowel it. They make a variety of cries and bloodcurdling howls, including a crazed laughing sound if under attack. The smaller, shy brown hyena *(Hyaena brunnea)* is found only in Southern Africa.

The magnificent sable antelope *(Hippotragus niger)* has a wonderful glossy coat – rust-red in females and jet-black in males. The males also sport massive, swept-back, scimitar-shaped horns that may exceed 3.3ft (1m) in length, and have fine bristling manes. Each herd moves in concert with a dominant bull that keeps guard. Lions are able to kill these antelope but show them a well-deserved respect – it is known that big cats have been gored to death by sable bulls.

Botswana birds and reptiles

There are over 500 different kinds of bird in Botswana, including ostriches, cormorants, African fish eagles, masked weavers, hornbills, and flamingos. Secretary birds *(Sagittarius serpentarius)* stalk the grassland, eating snakes whenever there is an opportunity. The Cape vulture *(Gyps coprotheres)* spreads its wings to a full 10ft (3m), rising on the hot air to glide, then swooping down at great speed if it spots a kill. A large flock of vultures can strip a carcass down to the bone in half an hour.

Reptiles are also plentiful in Botswana, and include crocodiles, pythons, geckos, tortoises, chameleons, black and green mambas, cobras, puff adders, and the boomslang *(Dispholidus typus)*. This highly poisonous tree-dwelling snake resides throughout subSaharan Africa. There are vast color variations in boomslangs but adult females are usually brown, and males a light green color with black or blue edges to their scales. Well-camouflaged in the foliage, they will strike without warning and deliver a highly potent venom via their large, deeply-grooved, folded fangs which will prove fatal if left untreated.

Namibia

Bordered by the Atlantic to the west, Namibia's climate ranges from subtropical to desert conditions. There are 26 parks and game reserves in Namibia, all containing abundant wildlife. The most famous is the Etosha National Park which protects lions, giraffe, and leopards. Eight endemic mammal species here include mice, gerbils, bats, and the black-faced impala *(Aepyceros melampus petersi)*. This is similar to the common impala but with a distinctive black stripe down its face. Here strides the elegant red hartebeest, warthogs trot along dusty tracks, gregarious flocks of red-billed hornbills *(Tockus erythrorhynchus)* forage for insects, seeds, scorpions, and small reptiles while the male lilac-breasted roller *(Coracias caudata)* flaunts its seven shades of blue plumage, sometimes rolling in mid-air to arouse female admiration. The hot sands of the Namibian desert dunes, for all their seemingly empty vastness, are busy with snakes and lizards, geckos, skinks, and the occasional ambling tortoise.

Lesotho

This name (it was formerly Basutoland) means the land of the people who speak Sotho. In the 1800s, it was ruled by a renowned chief, Moshoeshoe. It is the only independent country in the world which lies above 3300ft (1000m) in its entirety. In fact, 80 percent of the country rises higher than 5000ft (1800m). Lesotho is home to reedbuck and eland, baboons, rock hyraxes, mongoose, and meerkats. Its snakes include the shy but highly poisonous berg adder, and its birds include the bearded vulture, black eagle, and bald ibis.

Opposite: The spotted hyena lives south of the Sahara and is a dominant predator of Africa, as well as an eater of carrion. Lions account for some 50 percent of hyena deaths.

Left: Dating back some 80 million years, the Namib may be the oldest desert in the world.

Above: *Namibia: granite rocks flush scarlet in the sunrise. The quiver tree on the left is a branching succulent that thrives in this stony, desert domain and can sometimes reach a height of 20ft (6m). The young buds can be eaten and have a similar taste to asparagus.*
Left: *Clouds scudding above the sand dunes in Sossusvlei, which are some of the highest in Namibia – and the world. A huge clay pan here is enclosed by giant dunes, some of which rise to 1000ft (300m). Wind continually reshapes the patterns of these dunes in the Namib Desert.*

Previous pages: *Botswana: baobab trees against a fiery sky. Legend claims that their contorted shapes were caused by an angry deity plucking the tree from the ground and thrusting it back in again upside down!*

Above: *The highly venomous puff adder is quick to strike any intruder. Its potent venom rapidly destroys bloods cells.*

Above: *The stark shapes of petrified acacia trees in the Namib Desert, where cold Atlantic vapors meet searing hot desert. Thick fog often covers the dunes and tenebrionid beetles assume a head-down position so that condensing droplets of fog trickle down into their mouths. Another beetle,* Lepidochora discoidalis, *builds trenches to trap this moisture.*

Left: *Himba women cream their bodies with a rancid butterfat and ocher mix, scented with aromatic resin, to attain the desired intense red-bronze skin color. They adorn themselves with jewelry made from shells, iron, and rawhide.*

Right: *The 1800ft (550m) deep Fish River Canyon in Namibia is second in size only to the USA's Grand Canyon. The enormous gorge stretches for 100 miles (160km) and was probably formed about 500 million years ago.*

Swaziland

This small, landlocked country has a varied terrain comprising mountains, plateaus, and lowlands. Previously ruled by kings, including Mswati II who brought many different clans into the Swazi territory together to form one nation, it came under British rule from 1903 until 1968. The country is a constitutional monarchy, where the chosen king's son rules with his mother.

There are several nature reserves here, including the Mlawula Nature Reserve where white rhinos are protected. In the well-watered lowlands are swamps and lush plains. Tall grasses shelter gorgeous orchids and lilies, while ancient cycads flourish in shady spots. Birdlife is prolific with sunbirds and sugarbirds, blue cranes, swallows, and bald ibis. Herds of zebra, wildebeest, reedbuck, red hartebeest, and oribi graze the open grassland, while leopards, jackals, and bushpigs are careful to remain concealed.

The elusive serval cat *(Felis serval)* leads a solitary life once departed from the litter, and it establishes a territory up to 5sq miles (13km²) in area. They are of slender build, some 28-39in (70-100cm) from nose to rump, with long legs. Their excellent hearing means that they can even locate prey that is moving underground. Sadly, serval cat numbers are diminishing as their enemies include not only leopards, but also human hunters who seek to trade their exquisite fur.

Above: *The serval has huge erect ears and long legs. Its keen sight and acute hearing help it to detect prey in the tall grass while the spotted coat serves as good camouflage. It eats rodents, hares, hyraxes, and birds.*

Right: *In the late 1400s, the Swazi people crossed the Limpopo river and settled in southern Tsongaland. Their descendants today celebrate many traditional ceremonies and are wonderful dancers.*

The hyena-like aardwolf *(Proteles cristatus)* is a small and very furry animal that stands a mere 18in (46cm) tall at the shoulder. Its name, in Afrikaans, means 'earth wolf' and indeed it lives in underground burrows, emerging at intervals to mop up harvester termites and other insects with its long sticky tongue. Amazingly, a hungry aardwolf may eat up to 300,000 termites in a single night.

Aardvarks *(Orycteropus afer)* are found throughout Africa and these powerful diggers also relish a meal of termites which are caught on their long tongues as they excavate a termite mound. Also called earth pigs, aardvarks have long ears and are covered with bristly hairs. Their thick pink-gray skin is so tough that it protects them from insect bites.

The Republic of South Africa

For many centuries, the lure of South Africa's fine landscape and natural riches attracted many incomers, including the Dutch and British. Europeans arrived here from the 1600s and set about seizing both land and power. These colonial invaders were described by Zulus as being the 'color of pumpkin-porridge… rude of manners and without any graces or refinement. They carry a long stick of fire. With this they kill and loot.'

In 1797, the Dutch Boers trekked north to found their own republics. The discovery of diamonds in 1867 and gold in 1886 spurred greater immigration and a greed for wealth that intensified rivalry and resulted in the subjugation of the native inhabitants. Later, the Boers would resist the British, only to be defeated in the Boer War (1899-1902). The resulting Union of South Africa enshrined the dominance of the white settlers over the black population for much of the 20th century. However, the resistance of the black community and international political pressure eventually led to the establishment of the Republic of South Africa in 1994 under its first president, Nelson Mandela.

A long indented coastline stretches over 1555 miles (2500km) and faces both the Atlantic and Indian oceans, with the infamous Cape of Good Hope, where many a ship has foundered, lying between. It has a great variety of climates, from desert to semi-arid zones and subtropics. There are high mountains – a steep escarpment rises to an interior plateau and a sparsely populated scrubland. Its dramatic seaboard includes the lush eastern coastline. The extreme southwest – with its wet winters and hot, dry summers – is renowned for its fierce winds. The climate here is suitable, however, for producing good wine. Farther east on the country's south coast, there is enough rainfall all year to maintain a green landscape. This is called the Garden Route, and is a great place for spotting whales at certain times of the year. National parks include the Mala Mala Reserve which lies within Kruger National Park. The peaks of the Drakensberg Mountains rise to 10,000ft (3050m).

Right: Whales and dolphins often visit this beautiful stretch of coast near Yzerfontein on the Western Cape. Southern right whales migrate into these coastal waters to calve and nurse their young while humpbacks migrate through the region between May and December.

Right: South Africa has more than 1555 miles (2500km) of coastline, stretching from the edge of the Kalahari Desert in the northwest to the fertile St Lucia estuary in the northeast and fronting both the Atlantic and Indian oceans.

Above: The 'Whale Route' runs some 1555 miles (2500km) from south of Cape Town to Durban. This killer whale is spyhopping (popping its head out to look around). Whales often slap their tails on the surface of the water (known as 'lobtailing') and may breach by leaping rapidly out of the water and then splashing back into it.

Table Mountain is Cape Town's world-famous majestic landmark, sculpted over the centuries from sandstone and rising sharply to 3566ft (1087m) with its flat summit measuring nearly 1.9 miles (3km) across. Some of its rich fauna and flora may be found only here. There are some 1470 species of plants, including over 250 different daisies and the rare silver tree. Baboons, rock monitors, and porcupines scamper about its slopes, as do plump, furry rock hyraxes *(Procavia capensis)*, known locally as rock dassies. The little Table Mountain (or thumbed) ghost frog *(Heleophryne rosei)* is found nowhere else in the world. It lives in the clear flowing streams clinging to the rocks using widely spread, spatula-like, adhesive toes.

To the northwest is the Kalahari Gemsbok National Park and the red sands and scrub grasslands of the Kalahari Desert. In the northeast are the highveld plateau Bushveld region and the world-renowned Kruger National Park, established in 1898. The Kruger National Park is home to large numbers of hippopotamus, giraffes, zebras, buffaloes, warthogs, crocodiles, waterbuck, and antelopes. The impressive head count numbers some 12,000 elephants, 2500 buffaloes, 1500 lions, 1000 leopards, and 5000 rhinos – as well as numerous cheetahs, wild dogs, and spotted hyenas, and a great many reptiles and insects.

In air and sea

In the dry interior, warblers and larks sing, while bateleur and martial eagles soar above mountains and crags – also haunted by the Cape rockjumper. Spectacular birdlife includes tawny eagles, saddlebill storks, ground hornbills, ostriches, Cape parrots, orange-breasted sunbirds, Cape sugarbirds, protea seedeaters, and Hottentot buttonquails. There is a flourishing African (jackass) penguin colony at Boulders Beach National Park.

Meanwhile the seas that wash around the Cape offer unique opportunities to watch whales – including both the gloriously sleek black-and-white killer whale *(Orcinus orca)*, an efficient sharp-toothed predator that hunts as part of a co-operative pod, and the immense blue whale *(Balaenoptera musculus)*. Its staggering size makes this the largest animal ever to have lived on Earth. Some of these gentle giants have reached over 100ft (30m) in length but generally they are about 82ft (25m) from snout to their magnificent tail flukes. Placid and shy, they eat up to 8800lb (4 tonnes) of krill (small shrimp-like organisms) each day.

Hunted with harpoons relentlessly in the 1920s and 1930s (in 1931 alone about 30,000 of these beautiful, intelligent creatures were slaughtered), they are now on the brink of extinction. Those that survive seem to shame our cruelty with their exuberance for life as they make impressive 'headstands' before diving to 650ft (200m), and then 'blowing' when they resurface, sending jets of warm humid air almost 33ft (10m) into the air.

Left: Cape Town is famous for its unique penguin colony – and Table Mountain. The cableway there has, since 1929, carried more than 16 million visitors to the summit of a mountain that is home to some 1470 plant species – more than the entire total that the British Isles can claim!

Previous pages: Gemsbok – plus thousands of eland, blue wildebeest, red hartebeest, and springbok – roam in the Kalahari Gemsbok National Park. Above the rolling rust-red dunes and scattered grasses fly more than 200 species of birds, including many birds of prey. Black-maned Kalahari lions prowl the dry scrub and leopards hide in the branches of camelthorn trees.

Above: A misty sunrise on the Sand River, Mala Mala Game Reserve, Mpumalanga province, South Africa.
Opposite: A herd of eland are dwarfed by the mighty Giant's Castle and Drakensberg mountains in South Africa. Majestic bearded vultures haunt these skies.

Another giant in these waters is the formidable great white shark *(Carcharodon carcharias)* that may be seen breaching the surface or, for some intrepid divers, viewed from an underwater cage. Great whites are usually about 16ft (5m) long but they can grow up to 21ft (6.4m) in length. They use their 3000 or so fearsome triangular white teeth to slice off chunks of meat from their prey and swallow these whole. Depending on location, their diet includes fish, other sharks, rays, dolphins, and seals. After a substantial meal, the great white shark can last a month or two without needing to eat again.

The leatherback turtle *(Dermochelys coriacea)* has survived for more than 100 million years and is one of the world's largest living reptiles. It is known to cross the Atlantic and Pacific oceans in its extensive migratory travels. Loggerhead turtles *(Caretta caretta)* also swim in these seas. They too can cover vast distances, perhaps even the full 7500 miles (12,000km) across the Pacific Ocean, detecting wave direction and possibly using the Earth's magnetic field to navigate. These are the most common turtles seen off Southern Africa's coasts. Ocean currents transport them south, and some may spend five to ten years voyaging around Zanzibar, Madagascar, and Cape Agulhas.

Madagascar

The island of Madagascar has a unique ecology because over 80 percent of its animals are found nowhere else in the world. In Madagascar's rugged terrain and humid rainforests, where bloated leeches cling to intrepid explorers, a myriad strange creatures peep out from between the dripping leaves. Some ecologists have dubbed this island the eighth continent!

Sadly, over-zealous deforestation, shifting cultivation and livestock, gold and sapphire mining, and hunting has resulted in many species being eradicated. Today's survivors include the flat-tailed tortoise *(Pyxis planicauda)*, radiated tortoise *(Geochelone radiata)*, and the little hedgehog-like tenrec *(Tenrec ecaudatus)* that measures some 10-15in (25.5-38cm) long, and forages with its nose to the ground probing the forest litter and soil for insects and bugs. There are many colorful chameleons to be seen, including large turquoise varieties as well as jewel-eyed geckos and golden frogs. Plump, blood-red tomato frogs *(Dyscophus antongillii)* present an unbelievably bright splash of scarlet in the swamps and pools they inhabit, ready to inflate their body if disturbed.

The big-eyed aye-aye *(Daubentonia madagascariensis)* is the largest nocturnal primate in the world, and the only one known to use echolocation to find grubs as it taps a tree trunk with its elongated, slender middle finger. Once the aye-aye detects a hollow space inside the tree, it gnaws a hole in the wood and then extracts the hidden larvae using its amazingly long finger and claw. During mating, aye-ayes hang upside down on a branch for about an hour or so. A single offspring is the result of this union.

Lemurs are found only in Madagascar and the neighboring Comoros Islands. New-born infants are carried about in their mothers' mouths until they are old enough to hang on to her fur by themselves. They spend most of their time in trees and bushes, except for the ringtail lemur *(Lemur catta)* which scampers

about on the ground. They have big, bushy tails that they wave in the air as a form of communication and use for extra balance as they leap from tree to tree.

Attractive, agile sifakas (*Propithecus* sp.) with their golden staring eyes and tufted ears also live in the trees of Madagascar. They jump from one branch or tree to the next, using arms as long as their legs to help them swing along like acrobats before they stretch out for a rest. They are among some of the most threatened species on the planet and include the beautiful golden-crowned sifaka (*P. tattersalli*) and the silky sifaka (*P. candidus*) – a rare, all-white primate.

Some other animals of Southern Africa

South Africa's national fish, the galjoen *(Coracinus capensis)*, is found only along the South African coast, often in rough surf close to the shore. Its national animal is the springbok *(Antidorcas marsupialis)*, and this has also given its name to the South African rugby team. These antelope spring and leap about (behavior called pronking) in dry, barren areas and open grass plains. The blue crane *(Anthropoides paradisia)* is the national bird. It has a long neck, long legs, and elegant wing plumes. They lay their eggs in the bare veld, often close to water, and while they are usually quiet birds they can sometimes make loud high-pitched, rattling croaks.

Previous pages: The fruit-eating ring-tailed lemur lives in the forests and bush of southern Madagascar in troops up to 30 strong. They often run with their tails raised high like flags. The name 'lemur' means 'ghost' in the local language of Madagascar.

Below: Steam rises from the Sand River, Mala Mala, where animals gather to drink. The river flows north to south through the game reserve and draws herds of wildlife from miles around.

Above: The agile rock elephant shrew patrols pathways through the undergrowth, its little prehensile 'trunk' wriggling about in the search for insects like ants and termites – or seeds and juicy shoots. If alarmed, these shrews drum their feet and make high-pitched squeaks to alert one another.

Elephant shrews are found in many parts of Southern Africa, including the Namib Desert. With long muscular legs and elongated, mobile, trunk-like noses that sniff, twitch, and probe, these shy, strange-looking creatures are active mainly at dawn and dusk. They eat insects, seeds, and shoots, and are one of the rare three percent of mammals to be monogamous.

The fearless honey badger or ratel *(Mellivora capensis)* lives in the Kalahari Desert. They will seize snakes (including puff adders) in their jaws, taking care to grab them behind the head to kill them. They also ravage bees' nests in search of honey, sometimes in this pursuit enduring countless stings from the especially fierce African bees. They will attack scorpions, crocodiles, and porcupines without fear and it is even claimed by local tribes (although not yet scientifically proven) that any larger mammals – waterbuck, wildebeest, and even men – that provoke honey badgers may be fiercely seized by the scrotum and subjected to summary castration by these formidable little warriors!

Members of the mongoose family can be found in all parts of Africa south of the Sahara, including the banded, bushy-tailed, white-tailed, small gray, and marsh mongoose – not to mention the meerkat. A mongoose will tenaciously pursue its various types of prey, such as insects and scorpions, and is quite prepared to follow them into burrows if necessary. They are renowned for their nimble killing of snakes. Yellow mongooses *(Cynictis penicillata)* are distinct in having beautiful golden coats. These sleek, 16-24in (40-60cm) long creatures live in a communal burrow, sometimes shared with meerkats and ground squirrels, but they forage alone. Primarily insectivorous, like all of their kind they will tackle and eat highly venomous creatures.

Conclusion

Southern Africa is a place that assaults all the senses. It sings with color – there are lush green treetops, glistening foliage, vivid orange sand dunes where deserts meet the sea, scarlet sunsets, shimmering lakes, a land carpeted in golden daisies, orchids, and African violets.

Praying mantids abound in every hue from pale green to pink. There are orange-breasted sunbirds, gleaming olive terrapins, drifts of flamingos as pink as apple blossom, flaming scarlet frogs, and the smart black and white livery of jackass penguins *(Spheniscus demersus)* that strut about on islands between Namibia and Port Elizabeth, proud to be the only nesting penguins found on the African continent. They got the name because they bray like donkeys…

This is a magical place for sounds, too. Elephants trumpet on the savannah and lions roar in the bush. Somewhere there is the rhythmic beat of a drum, cicadas thrum, waves crash on the shore and, every now and then, whales thrash the ocean with their great, gleaming tail flukes.

Sometimes the air quivers with the heat on the plains … sometimes it slips warm and moist into the forests … or rises in great thunderclouds above the towering mountain peaks.

This place is many wonderful things. This is Africa.

Left: Lower Zambezi National Park on the Zambezi River in Zambia is home to some of Africa's largest elephant herds (up to a hundred strong). They are often seen at the river's edge, as are buffalo, waterbuck, and fish eagles. Here an elephant cools off in the river.

Above: An aardvark cautiously emerges from its burrow at dusk. It generally stays at the entrance, checking that all is safe, before suddenly leaping out. Then it stops again, rises up on its hind legs, perks up its ears, and peers all around. After a few more big leaps, it will amble off to look for a termite mound to plunder for food.

Right: A Cape cobra in the Kalahari Desert. This small, slender snake is possibly the most venomous African cobra. It does not spit venom but its bite can cause paralysis and then death in just 30 minutes. Nervous and aggressive, it reacts to a threat by rearing up, hissing, spreading its broad hood, and advancing on an intruder.

Above: *Mpumalanga, South Africa: in Bourke's Luck Potholes (named for a gold miner) the whirling waters have ground surreal cylindrical holes out of the bedrock.*

Left: *A herd of white rhinos graze the veld in the Mala Mala Game Reserve, Mpumalanga. The unfenced border between Mala Mala and the Kruger Park allows herds of animals to migrate unhindered to the perennial Sand River which flows north to south through the reserve for 28 miles (45km).*

Left: *The dainty springbok can be found all over the dry savannah of Southern Africa. Here fighting males clash horns. They can run at 50mph (80km/h) and are famous for their high jumps (known as pronking) when they leap up and down like bouncing balls.*

Above: *Sable antelope in Kruger National Park. These large, handsome animals live in wooded savannah and have shaggy manes, white bellies and face markings, and long ridged horns. Males have glossy black coats; females are chestnut to dark brown.*

Top: The beautiful lilac-breasted roller is named for its acrobatic rolling courtship flight. It eats grasshoppers, beetles, and lizards, plus crabs and small amphibians.

Above: The yellow-billed hornbill has striped and spotted plumage. It eats seeds, insects, spiders, scorpions, termites, and ants.

Left: The Sentinel in Free State's Golden Gate Highlands National Park. The birds of prey that soar over the golden and ocher sandstone cliffs and outcrops include bearded vultures, Cape vultures, and martial eagles. The numerous caves in the sandstone rocks were once shelters for the bushmen. Many of their cave paintings are well preserved.

Above: *Johannesburg – the capital of Gauteng, South Africa's smallest province – is the financial, economic, and cultural center of South Africa. It was founded in 1886 as a result of gold being discovered in the region.*

Facts and figures

Figures vary, depending on the sources, and obviously some (such as populations) are constantly subject to change, but the following facts provide a few fascinating snippets about the geography, people, and animals of Africa:

Geography

• Africa comprises 53 independent countries and is almost completely encircled by water.

• Africa is the second largest continent in the world, after Asia. It measures over 11,700,000sq miles (30,300,000km²).

• Africa occupies about 20 percent of the Earth's total land area and is three times the size of Europe.

• Africa's coastline runs for 18,976 miles (30,539km).

• The continent's greatest length from north to south is around 5000 miles (8000km).

• The river Nile is the world's longest, at about 4160 miles (6695km).

• The Sahara is the world's largest desert — it is so huge that it is larger than the continental US.

• Africa's highest point is Mount Kilimanjaro in Tanzania at 19,331ft (5892m).

• Africa's lowest point is Lake Assal in Djibouti at more than 492ft (150m) below sea level.

• The largest country in Africa is Sudan, at 967,500sq miles (2,505,800km²).

• Africa's largest lake is Victoria. At over 26,600sq miles (68,800km²) this is the world's second-largest freshwater lake after North America's Lake Superior.

• The smallest mainland African state is the Gambia, covering an area of 4363sq miles (11,300km²).

• Lake Tanganyika is the deepest lake in Africa reaching 4710ft (1436m) — the second deepest freshwater lake in the world, after Russia's Lake Baikal.

• The Great African Rift Valley runs for 3000 miles (4828km) from Syria in the Middle East to Mozambique in south-eastern Africa.

People

• The total population of Africa is estimated at some 890,000,000 people, and is increasing at 3 percent per year — faster than any other part of the world. It may reach 1.8 billion by 2050.

• Over one-tenth of the world's population live in Africa, which is about one-fifth of the globe's total land area.

• An estimated 1000 languages and dialects are spoken in Africa.

• Africa includes the 15 least developed nations in the world. 70 percent of its population survives on earnings of less than $2 a day.

• Africa's largest city is Cairo, in Egypt, with a population of 15 million people.

• Most Africans are either Muslim or Christian. Both Christianity and Islam have been adapted to incorporate elements of the traditional religions (such as voodoo) that play such an important part in many Africans' lives. These religions involve prayer and sacrifice and have often spearheaded political change, with revolts against both European and African rulers and chiefs.

• Apart from Muslim nations, Ghana has the lowest per capita consumption of beer in Africa.

• 3000 children under the age of five die each day from malaria in Africa.

• 17 million people in sub-Saharan Africa have died of AIDS — and at least 25 million people in Africa are HIV-positive.

• Nigeria is the most densely populated country in Africa with more than 130 million inhabitants.

• There are more people with internet access in New York City, in the USA, than on the entire continent of Africa.

Animals

• Four of the world's five fastest land animals live in Africa. The cheetah is fastest at 70mph (113km/h), with wildebeest, lion, and Thomson's gazelle next — all capable of reaching about 50mph (80km/h) over short distances.

• An ostrich is the world's largest and heaviest living bird at 9ft (2.75m) tall, and weighing up to 345lb (156.5kg). Each huge eye is bigger than its brain.

• The low frequency 'song' of the blue whale is, at 188 decibels, the loudest sound made by any animal.

• The goliath frog, the world's biggest, is found in Cameroon. It can grow up to 13in (33cm) in length, and weighs up to 7lb (3kg).

• The African elephant is the largest living land mammal. A male elephant's head and body length, including trunk, measures about 16.4 to 23 feet (5–7m) with a 4ft (1.2m) tail. With a shoulder height of 10 to 13 feet (3–4m), it weighs in at a mighty 7 to 9 tons.

• The tallest animal on Earth is the giraffe. A male's horn tops are approximately 18.7ft (5.7m) above ground level.

• No two zebras have stripes that are exactly identical.

• A camel has a tough mouth; the inside is so resilient that when it eats a thorny twig, the sharp points do not pierce it. It can digest bones, fish, meat, leather — and even the fabric of canvas tents.

• The hippopotamus often gives birth under water and then suckles its young in a lake or river.

• Chimpanzees rarely live past the age of 50 in the wild, but have been known to reach the age of 60 in captivity.

Index

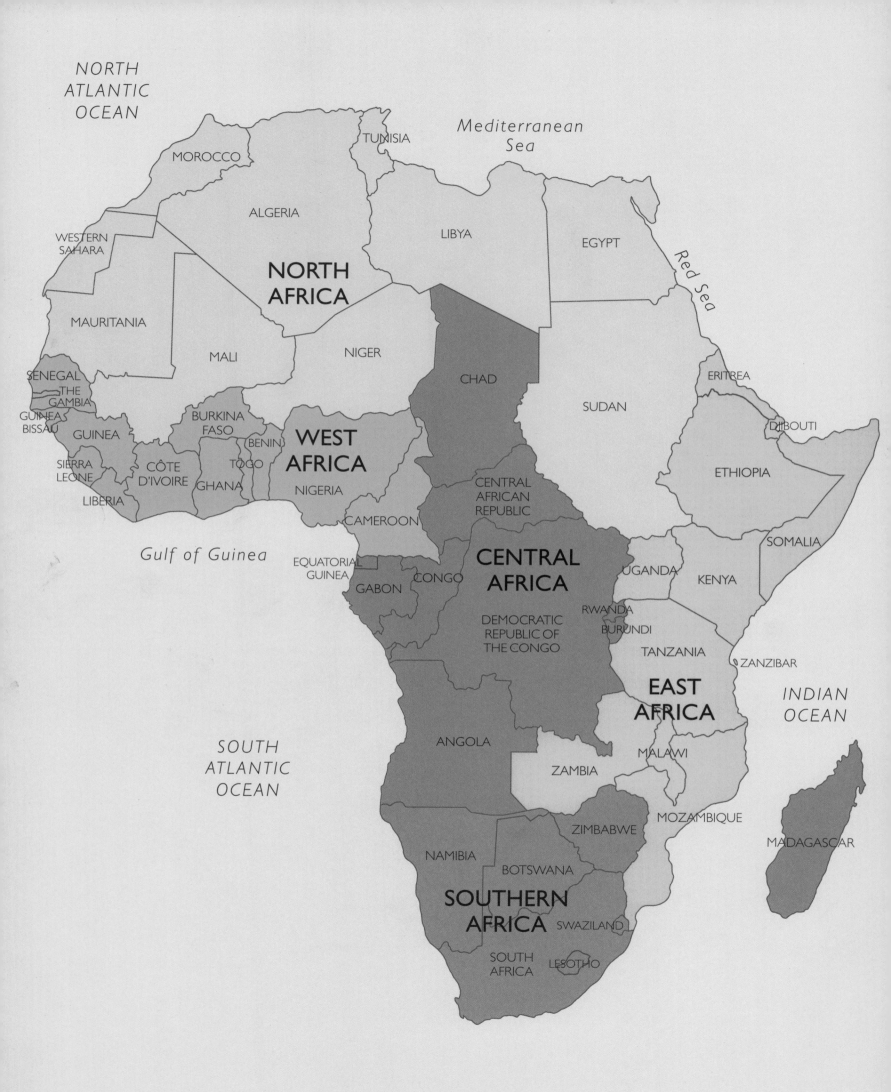